DATE DUE

THE LIBRARY STORE   #47-0120

CONTINUOUS QUALITY IMPROVEMENT IN HIGHER EDUCATION

CONTINUOUS QUALITY IMPROVEMENT IN HIGHER EDUCATION

John Robert Dew and
Molly McGowan Nearing

OUACHITA TECHNICAL COLLEGE

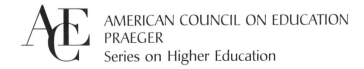

AMERICAN COUNCIL ON EDUCATION
PRAEGER
Series on Higher Education

Library of Congress Cataloging-in-Publication Data

Dew, John R.
    Continuous quality improvement in higher education / John Robert Dew and
Molly McGowan Nearing.
        p. cm. — (ACE/Praeger series on higher education)
    Includes bibliographical references and index.
    ISBN 0–275–98389–7 (alk. paper)
        1. Universities and colleges—United States—Administration. 2. Total quality
management in higher education—United States. I. Nearing, Molly McGowan.
II. Title. III. American Council on Education/Praeger series on higher education.
LB2341.D47   2004
378.1'07—dc22   2004041571

British Library Cataloguing in Publication Data is available.

Library of Congress Catalog Card Number: 2004041571
ISBN: 0–275–98389–7

First published in 2004

Praeger Publishers, 88 Post Road West, Westport, CT 06881
An imprint of Greenwood Publishing Group, Inc.
www.praeger.com

Printed in the United States of America

The paper used in this book complies with the
Permanent Paper Standard issued by the National
Information Standards Organization (Z39.48–1984).

10 9 8 7 6 5 4 3 2 1

CONTENTS

ACKNOWLEDGMENTS

The authors wish to thank many people who have been their teachers and who have been trailblazers in implementing continuous improvement in higher education. Among the teachers are Dr. John Peters, Dr. Malcolm Knowles, Dr. W. Edwards Deming, Dr. Joseph Juran, Mr. Benjamin Tregoe, Mr. Paulo Freire, and Mr. Myles Horton.

Among the trailblazers are Dr. John Harris at Samford University, Dr. Susan Williams at Belmont University, Ms. Louise Sandmeyer at Pennsylvania State University, Ms. Maury Cotter at the University of Wisconsin–Madison, Dr. Brent Ruben at Rutgers University, and Mr. Jim Spring at Binghamton University. Special recognition goes to Dr. Charles Sorensen who serves as chancellor at the University of Wisconsin–Stout, the first university to win the Malcolm Baldrige National Quality Award.

Among the outstanding leaders in higher education, the authors wish to thank President Lois DeFleur at Binghamton University, Dr. Andrew Sorensen at the University of South Carolina, and Dr. Robert Witt at The University of Alabama for their vision and commitment to continuous improvement.

Special thanks goes to Louise Sandmeyer and Maury Cotter for their reading and comments on this manuscript.

Although neither Binghamton University nor The University of Alabama is accredited by the Higher Learning Commission of the North Central Association, the authors wish to acknowledge the groundbreaking work of Dr. Stephen Spangehl and his team in developing the Alternative

Quality Improvement Process and the excellent support given to that project by the Pew Charitable Trusts.

The University of Alabama is indebted to the Alfred P. Sloan Foundation for its early support of continuous improvement and to the Boeing Corporation, Milliken, Federal Express, and the Ritz-Carlton Hotels for their guidance in developing a continuous improvement methodology.

PREFACE

We have two objectives in preparing this book. The first is to provide leaders in the higher education community with a frame work in which to understand and apply Continuous Improvement theory and methods in a widely diverse range of higher education institutions.

We recognize that the great variation among higher education institutions, coupled with the wide range of approaches to Continuous Improvement, can present the mistaken impression that there may not be a defined body of knowledge from which to draw to design and guide the journey toward excellence in the context of specific institutions. In the design and development of Continuous Improvement methods on our campuses, we have found a solid body of knowledge that will add value to leaders in any higher education setting.

Recognizing that each campus works on its journey toward excellence with a unique history and context, our second objective is to provide a wide variety of examples of effective practices that campuses can employ related to strategic planning, self-assessments, benchmarking, building a collaborative campus culture, engaging faculty and staff in team activities, using measurement and feedback systems, and applying Continuous Improvement concepts to improving teaching and learning in the classroom.

HOW TO NAVIGATE THIS BOOK

The first chapter offers a perspective on how Continuous Improvement has developed over time to a point where it is now being embedded in the re-accreditation process for many higher education associations, such as the Higher Learning Commission of the North Central Association, the Southern Association for Colleges and Schools, and the Middle States Commission on Higher Learning. The chapter provides some historical perspective on institutions that were early pioneers in Continuous Improvement and the growth of interest in these concepts and methods.

Chapter Two provides a variety of models and perspectives for framing Continuous Improvement in the higher education context. The chapter offers a phase model for the introduction, growth and maturity of Continuous Improvement concepts on a campus, and includes specific examples form a diverse selection of campuses.

Chapter Three offers perspectives on introducing Continuous Improvement concepts, such as process variation, process improvement, and the concept of the vital few, to the campus. This chapter includes examples of how various campuses have conducted Continuous Improvement workshops, developed facilitators, engaged faculty, and shared information about their successes.

Chapter Four provides perspectives on the nature of self-assessments and the rapidly growing use of approaches based on Continuous Improvement concepts, such as the Malcolm Baldrige National Quality Award and new regional re-accreditation models. This chapter will help readers appreciate the manner in which self-assessments are changing from a quality assurance approach to a Continuous Improvement approach.

Chapter Five addresses the issue of strategic planning from a Continuous Improvement perspective. This chapter offers guidelines for a strategic planning method based on the "future search" method that is highly effective in higher education settings, along with examples of strategic planning methods used at a variety of institutions.

Chapter Six examines the practice of benchmarking, which has a somewhat different meaning in the Continuous Improvement vocabulary than has traditionally been used in higher education. The chapter provides a comparison of the types of benchmarking that will benefit a campus, along with practical steps to follow.

Chapter Seven explores issues related to building a collaborative culture among faculty and staff that is essential for establishing and sustaining a culture of Continuous Improvement. The chapter presents some practical implications of the impact of different leadership styles, the meaning and method of achieving consensus, how to resolve problems inherent in meetings, and a brief, but practical introduction to the phase theory of groups. The chapter also provides a quick introduction to the use of 360 degree feedback instruments as a method to improve communication in various campus settings.

Chapter Eight addresses some nuts and bolts issues of Continuous Improvement by considering the various approaches to forming and using teams to improve the academic and administrative systems on campus. This includes the use of cross-functional teams, natural work teams, student teams, and the distinction between teams and committees. The chapter provides examples of the use of tools unique to Continuous Improvement to bring a fresh perspective to analyzing campus issues, and also provides some useful perspective on the theory of empowerment and endullment in the educational setting.

Chapter Nine brings some structure to the chaotic issue of measurement and feedback in the higher education setting. The chapter constructs a taxonomy of measurement based on the Continuous Improvement "Input-Process-Output" model. Examples drawn from a wide variety of campuses provide insights on how to obtain stakeholder feedback using surveys and focus groups. This chapter also provides an introduction to the important concept of the Balanced Score Card for tracking institutional performance.

This book concludes with Chapter Ten, which offers examples of the application of Continuous Improvement concepts to improving academic programs through curriculum redesign and improvement of individual classes.

John Robert Dew and Molly McGowan Nearing

CHAPTER 1

The Development of Continuous Improvement in Higher Education

Higher Education has a remarkable opportunity to model for its customers high standards of responsiveness.
— Thomas Corts, President, Samford University

In this book, continuous improvement refers to a body of knowledge, developed both inside and outside of the academic community over the past seventy-five years, that focuses on learning how a system functions and on improving the performance of the system. The system can be educational, manufacturing, governmental, health care, or any service being provided.

Within the context of the academic community, continuous improvement is the body of knowledge that helps us learn how to better facilitate the learning that occurs through teaching and research. Continuous improvement addresses learning processes as well as all the administrative processes necessary to support students, faculty, alumni, and other stakeholders in the higher education setting.

Although it is possible to trace the origins of continuous improvement back to the standardized measurements employed by the Egyptians in building the pyramids, continuous improvement, as a systematic body of knowledge, did not begin to take shape until the work of Walter Shewhart. Shewhart was both an academic, on the faculty at the Stevens Institute of Technology, and a researcher at Bell Laboratories. Shewhart focused on developing statistical methods to reduce the variation in manufactured items, publishing his work in 1931 in *Economic Control of Quality in Manu-factured Product*. Shewhart invented statistical charts that could help manufacturers see patterns of variation and understand how variation influences the final outcome of any process.

During the 1930s and 1940s, the body of knowledge began to incorporate other statistical concepts, such as sampling, and embraced practical tools and concepts developed within the engineering community. W. Edwards Deming, who taught at New York University, became a champion of Shewhart's statistical control charts and introduced the concept to the Japanese. Joseph Juran developed new concepts, such as the Pareto analysis, and began to organize and teach the concepts as a body of knowledge.

In the 1950s and 1960s, continuous improvement expanded to include concepts and tools from the social sciences and organizational development. Tools such as force field analysis, affinity diagrams, and brainstorming became integrated with the statistical methods. Improvement efforts began to focus increasingly on the use of teams to diagnose and improve processes. Many new contributions came from Japan, including statistical tools and the use of group problem-solving methods developed by Kaoru Ishikawa. As in the United States, the expansion of continuous improvement concepts in Japan was a collaborative effort between academics and their colleagues who applied and tested new statistical and group problem-solving methods in the field.

Continuous improvement has grown to include many new concepts since Shewhart's early work. It includes the statistical understanding of process variation, concepts related to group dynamics developed in the social sciences, and action research theories developed by academics working in a wide range of adult learning contexts. Continuous improvement has provided a dynamic opportunity for praxis related to systems theory and field research.

The interdisciplinary nature of continuous improvement as a body of knowledge accounts for the diverse manner in which it is taught within the academic community. In some universities, research and classes related to continuous improvement are taught in the business school, often with an emphasis on statistics. On other campuses, continuous improvement courses reside primarily in the school of engineering. Schools of education offer their own approach, known as action research. Academic programs in health care are increasingly using the continuous improvement concepts, as are academic programs in human environmental sciences and public administration.

One of the myths concerning continuous improvement is that the concepts originated within the business community and carry cultural connotations that are inappropriate for the academy. The body of knowledge for continuous improvement evolved over many decades through the collaboration of academics and their students who sought to apply these concepts in business and industry. In many cases, the use of continuous improvement concepts were strongly resisted by business managers who did not want to yield to new ways of thinking that often seemed like an intrusion of academics into the business world. Early pioneers in continuous improvement often divided their careers between the university and applied research centers with companies such as Bell Laboratories.

W. Edwards Deming worked with Shewhart and taught thousands in seminars on applying continuous improvement concepts through George Washington University. In addition to his consulting work with government and industry, Deming taught graduate courses at New York University for several decades. Deming began encouraging faculty and staff in higher education to study the continuous improvement concepts in order to establish a methodology for improvement of academic programs in the late 1980s.

THE GROWTH OF CONTINUOUS IMPROVEMENT IN HIGHER EDUCATION

Support for continuous improvement in higher education has grown from a unique combination of circumstances in the late 1980s and early 1990s. At that time, the national focus on continuous improvement was at its highest peak since the Second World War, when quality methods had ensured the reliability of the immense volume of materials produced for the war effort. A new national award for excellence in management systems (The Malcolm Baldrige National Quality Award) had just been created in the late 1980s, and many states were organizing state-level awards and quality centers. Many companies were achieving success by focusing on continuous improvement, and their CEOs were recognizing a need to imbed the quality concepts into the undergraduate and graduate curriculum in higher education. Non-profit organizations were also interested in supporting the use of continuous improvement concepts to improve all levels of education.

In this rich mixture of interests and events, a variety of campuses began to experiment with continuous improvement principles and to design quality initiatives for a wide range of reasons. Community colleges, private colleges and universities, large public universities, and regional universities began to develop approaches that applied concepts drawn from the quality discipline.

It is difficult to attempt to summarize this movement out of concern for leaving out an important campus or individual, but a quick sketch will be useful for understanding how continuous improvement has evolved on various campuses.

COMMUNITY COLLEGES

Several community colleges began developing approaches for using quality principles that fit well with their mission and needs in the late 1980s and early 1990s.

Western Wisconsin Technical College (WWTC) began exploring the work of Dr. W. Edwards Deming in 1988. With the selection of Dr. Lee Rasch as president in 1989, WWTC launched a campus continuous improvement initiative, provided training for faculty and staff, and organized improvement teams. WWTC has pioneered many innovative approaches to continuous improvement and used the Wisconsin Forward Award application in 1999 to conduct a campuswide self-assessment. WWTC's early work in continuous improvement positioned it to quickly adopt the North Central Association's Alternate Quality Improvement Process in 2001.

Fox Valley Technical College (FVTC), in Appleton, Wisconsin, was another early leader in quality, using continuous improvement tools for planning new academic programs. FVTC created more than fifty improvement teams by 1992.

The Eastern Iowa Community College District, comprising three campuses, launched a continuous improvement initiative in 1992 and 1993, and worked with other colleges to establish the Continuous Quality Improvement Network (CQIN), which has developed quality-based self-assessment tools.

Many other community colleges came on board with improvement initiatives in the late 1990s. Community colleges often provide quality workshops for their local communities and are frequent partners with local sections of the American Society for Quality (ASQ) for quality-related training, so there are many opportunities for community college leaders to learn about continuous improvement principles and methods. Community colleges are often involved in helping regional organizations prepare and compete for state-level continuous improvement awards, so it is logical for them to become engaged with quality improvement. Lakeshore Technical College, for example, applied for the Wisconsin Forward Award in 2000 and has developed a quality-based strategic planning model.

PRIVATE COLLEGES

Continuous improvement among private colleges and universities may have started in 1989 when Bill Trout, president of Belmont University, attended a seminar with Dr. Deming. In 1990, Dr. Trout had most of Belmont's deans attend a Deming seminar and established a Center for Quality at Belmont. Belmont won the prestigious Tennessee Quality Award in 1993 and played an important role in the development of a version of the Malcolm Baldrige National Quality Award for Education and in the development of the quality-based revisions to the Southern Association of Colleges and Schools' reaccreditation process.

Concurrently, Samford University in Birmingham, Alabama, began its "Student First Quality Quest" under the leadership of Dr. Thomas Corts. Samford obtained a Fund for Improvement of Post-Secondary Education (FIPSE) grant in 1990 to help launch its continuous improvement initiative, which applied continuous improvement methods to academic programs and administrative activities. Dr. John Harris and Dr. Mark Baggett collaborated with the faculty at Samford, Belmont, and The University of Alabama to produce the first broad account of a quality improvement methodology for a campus, *Quality Quest in the Academic Process*, published in 1992.

Samford and Belmont were instrumental in sharing their quality model with other institutions throughout the 1990s. Dr. Corts subsequently led the effort to integrate continuous improvement concepts into the SACS reaccreditation model.

Babson College, in Massachusetts, developed a continuous improvement program in 1992 under the leadership of a president who was a former vice chair of Xerox Corporation. Babson's initiative was organized by Susan West Engelkemeyer and quickly migrated from a focus on individual improvement teams to a systemic assessment of the institution's management system using the Baldrige criteria.

Villanova University established its continuous improvement initiative in 1993 with a quality steering committee. The members began conducting orientation and training sessions during the summer of 1993 and soon had a vibrant program working on dozens of initiatives. Those dozens have grown into hundreds over the past nine years.

The University of Miami (Florida) likewise initiated a continuous improvement initiative in the early 1990s. The Miami initiative focused on projects and processes in the Financial Affairs area, where the university has developed one of the best sets of performance measures for financial and support processes in the country.

PUBLIC UNIVERSITIES

The continuous improvement initiative in large public universities like-wise emerged in the late 1980s. Pennsylvania State University was faced with the prospect of losing $40 million in state appropriations and began investigating ways to improve performance. While studying Deming's ideas, Penn State turned to Oregon State University for its initial train-ing on continuous improvement and eventually settled on Dr. Joseph Juran's approach for organizing a quality initiative and used the Juran On Quality video series to expand quality training on its campus. Penn State's continuous improvement initiative continued to grow into hundreds of successful improvement projects, leading it to pilot the concept of a campus continuous improvement forum to showcase its successes.

The University of Wisconsin–Madison launched a continuous improve-ment initiative at almost the same time, when Dr. Donna Shalala decided to start an organized effort to eliminate long student lines and to improve administrative processes. The next chancellor, Dr. David Ward, saw the importance of integrating continuous improvement with strategic plan-ning and the benefits of applying continuous improvement concepts to academic programs. UW–Madison was also able to make effective use of local resources to grow its quality initiative, since the Madison area hosted the Hunter Conference, one of the country's top annual gathering of qual-ity professionals. Madison, in the late 1980s and early 1990s, was also home to one of the country's largest quality consulting organizations led by Brian Joiner. Like Penn State, UW–Madison's continuous improve-ment initiative has resulted in hundreds of improvements in academic and administrative processes and the close integration of quality management and strategic planning.

Oregon State University (OSU) began looking at the work of Deming and Juran in 1990 and invited Deming to the campus to speak. OSU es-tablished ten initial teams and conducted many successful improvement projects. Under the leadership of Edwin Coate, vice president for Finance and Administration, OSU created a continuous improvement model that identified critical processes and an analysis of quality issues in higher education that were ten years ahead of most other campuses. OSU iden-tified twenty campuses that were piloting continuous improvement ini-tiatives in 1991. Through a telephone survey, OSU found that 70 percent of these schools had continuous improvement teams in administrative areas, and 45 percent had them in academic areas. Unfortunately, OSU's leadership lacked what Deming called "constancy of purpose." With changes in leadership, the continuous improvement initiative at OSU faded into history.

Rutgers University organized an internal assessment of administrative practices in 1991, resulting in the establishment of a university-wide continuous improvement initiative in 1992.

Purdue University launched its continuous improvement initiative in 1992 with over 100 administrators attending quality improvement training at Motorola. Purdue has maintained a continuous improvement focus for a decade, renewing its initiative in the late 1990s as the Excellence 21 program.

The University of California–Berkeley launched its continuous improvement initiative in the mid-1990s with strong input from the University of Wisconsin–Madison. Berkeley has developed a four-tiered approach to continuous improvement:

1. Strategic leadership and vision
2. Organizational assessment
3. Process improvement
4. Staff engagement

This comprehensive approach has led to a wide variety of academic and administrative improvement initiatives.[1] Many other major public universities, such as Binghamton University, The University of Alabama, and the University of Michigan, began continuous improvement initiatives in the mid-1990s, learning from the successful programs at UW–Madison, Penn State, Villanova, Belmont, Samford, and Rutgers.

REGIONAL PUBLIC UNIVERSITIES

Several public regional universities rose to national prominence for their leadership in applying quality concepts in higher education throughout the 1990s. Because of their size and mission, regional universities, like private institutions, are often better positioned than large research universities to embrace the broad concept of a quality management system, as described in the Baldrige Award, or in state-level quality programs that are based on the Baldrige criteria.

No campus in the country has gone further than the University of Wisconsin–Stout, the first university to win the Baldrige Award. Under the leadership of Dr. Charles Sorensen, UW–Stout has developed a comprehensive management system for its entire campus that fully embraces the continuous improvement concepts. Although many campuses have been successful with process improvements, integrating quality and strategic planning, the use of performance measures, or the use of continuous improvement methods to improve core academic processes, UW–Stout is the first to combine all these in a sustained, systematic approach.

Other regional universities, such as Northwestern Missouri and the University of Missouri at Rolla, have been successful with using state-level quality award programs to structure their continuous improvement activities. It is likely that regional universities like these and others in the California State University system will be among the next to win a Baldrige Award.

UNIVERSITY SYSTEMS

In the mid-1990s, the California State University (CSU) System launched a major effort to bring continuous improvement methods simultaneously to multiple campuses across a major university system. Under the leadership of Dr. Charles Reed, the CSU System established a Quality Improvement Planning Committee with representatives from campuses all across the state. CSU has introduced continuous improvement methods on over a dozen campuses. Moreover, the CSU System has developed surveys, performance measures, and balanced score cards for administrative processes that facilitate comparison of performance between campuses and the sharing of effective practices.

California State University initiated an Annual Quality Improvement Program in 1999 that is held in different cities around the state each year. As in the continuous improvement forums initiated at Penn State, teams from campuses from across California share success stories and performance data.

PATTERNS OF SUCCESS AND FAILURE

Not all the early efforts to establish continuous improvement efforts in higher education were successful. Many early efforts failed to connect continuous improvement with the core processes in higher education— teaching and research. Bonvillian and Dennis have recounted the problems they encountered at the Rochester Institute of Technology due to the focus on administrative processes and the omission of work on the teaching and learning processes.[2] Writing about activities at Shippensburg University, Waters noted that empowerment efforts, as part of the campus's continuous improvement efforts, often failed because of little campus investment in training employees to understand and use continuous improvement methods.[3] A continuous improvement effort launched at George Washington University in 1991 stalled out due to a lack of well-planned assessment of the institution for opportunities for improvement and through the use of quality consultants who were not knowledgeable of the academic culture.[4] Many institutions have attempted to begin a continuous improvement initiative but have run into the problem, reported by Wheatley at the University of West Florida, of a turnover in academic leadership that interrupts the constancy of purpose necessary for success in continuous improvement.[5]

QUALITY CENTERS AND CAMPUS QUALITY

Several universities have well-recognized centers that foster continuous improvement–related research and provide consulting and public workshops on continuous improvement to corporations, government agencies, and healthcare providers.

While some of these centers have had a duel focus on providing consulting support internal and external to their respective campuses, many of these centers have not played a significant role, so far, in establishing a continuous improvement focus on their campus. One notable exception is the Center for Organizational Development and Leadership at Rutgers University, under the leadership of Dr. Brent Ruben. Ruben has combined research and consulting on continuous improvement in the private sector with the internal continuous initiative at Rutgers. Through his involvement with the National Association of College and University Business Officers (NACUBO), Ruben led the creation of the National Consortium for Continuous Improvement in Higher Education (NCCI). NCCI now has over fifty research universities, regional universities, and private universities and colleges as member institutions and conducts an annual conference on continuous improvement in higher education.

It is a curious fact that many faculty members with expertise in the management and engineering disciplines at institutions across the country have not engaged their administrations in applying the continuous principles. Numerous institutions have tremendous untapped expertise that can help them make significant improvement.

A noteworthy exception to this is Dr. Howard Gitlow at the University of Miami in Florida. Dr. Gitlow was one of Dr. Deming's graduate students and has worked with the university's administration for a decade in developing performance measures for administrative processes.

The newest center at a major university is the Juran Center for Leadership in the Carlson School of Management at the University of Minnesota. Dr. Juran earned his B.S. in Engineering from the University of

Minnesota in 1924 and has given his alma mater his collection of case studies and writings on quality improvement that spans more than seventy years. The Juran Center for Leadership sponsored a Quality Summit in 2002 with corporate quality leaders, researchers, and quality directors from several universities called in to evaluate the current state of the quality movement and to define research needs for supporting continued expansion of the use of quality methods.

CORPORATE ENCOURAGEMENT AND SUPPORT

Many corporations have encouraged higher education to embrace continuous improvement principles because of the positive impact that continuous improvement methods have had in their own performances. They would like to see K–12 and higher education improve and know that the quality methods actually work in helping to improve planning, work processes, stakeholder buy-ins, employee involvement, and measurement and control of an organization.

Several companies banded together in 1988 to form the TQM (Total Quality Management) Forum, designed to encourage universities to integrate the quality concepts into the undergraduate curriculum.

In 1991, IBM launched its TQM Competition, providing eight awards of either $1 million cash or $3 million in IBM equipment to campuses interested in quality. Two hundred and four universities applied, and nine were selected. Two of these nine were UW–Madison and Penn State, which have sustained their commitment to quality for over a decade.

The TQM University Challenge, funded by IBM, Milliken, Motorola, Proctor and Gamble, and Xerox, provided major grants to universities that would pilot campus Total Quality Management initiatives and integrate quality into the curriculum. Twenty-seven research universities submitted proposals and eight universities were selected.

Corporations have continued to support community colleges, private colleges, and regional and national public universities when campuses ask for their help. Baldrige Award–winning companies, such as Milliken, Motorola, Boeing, Federal Express, and Ritz-Carlton, have continued to provide advice and assistance to schools engaged in the quality journey.

NON-PROFIT ORGANIZATIONS

Several non-profit organizations have also been supporters of the continuous improvement initiative in higher education.

The American Association for Higher Education (AAHE) launched a Continuous Quality Improvement Project in 1993. The project produced a bibliography of publications on continuous improvement at campuses across the nation and produced a booklet profiling activities at twenty-five institutions in the early 1990s.

The American Society for Quality has organized an Education Division that includes faculty members who teach quality at many institutions. Although the Education Division has primarily focused on implementing quality methods in K–12 schools and has developed the nationally recognized Koality Kids program, it is also supportive of continuous improvement initiatives in higher education. The ASQ maintains many campus chapters, primarily for students majoring in business and engineering.

GOAL/QPC, a non-profit education, training, and publishing center in Massachusetts, has helped provide training to a wide variety of campuses and published Samford University's book on campus quality. Mr. Bob King, with GOAL/QPC, continues to support continuous improvement programs in higher education and has volunteered his time to lead workshops at NCCI conferences.

The NACUBO has been a strong advocate of the use of quality tools to improve administrative processes on campus. Business officers maintain contact with their counterparts in the private sector and are aware of the benefits of quality methods in reducing costs and improving service. The NACUBO has encouraged continuous improvement facilitators from many campuses to work together to share information and methods in order to help more schools adopt a quality management system.

ACCREDITING ORGANIZATIONS

There is a growing movement to add value to the traditional quality assurance function of reaccreditation by adding a quality improvement component or even entirely replacing quality assurance with quality improvement. The fact is, few schools that undergo the rigors of a quality assurance–oriented self-study and assessment are in any risk of not being reaccredited and are not often motivated by this process to make improvements. The Higher Learning Commission of the North Central Association has launched the Academic Quality Improvement Process (AQIP) under the leadership of Stephen Spangehl. The AQIP offers institutions an alternate path based on quality improvement, integrating self-assessment, strategic planning, and quality tools and methods for reaccreditation.

The Southern Association of Colleges and Schools (SACS) has revised their reaffirmation process for higher education to include the expectation that schools will develop systematic approaches to quality improvement.

The SACS now requires each school to develop a Quality Enhancement Plan that requires a major, systematic project to improve student-learning outcomes. The Middle States Commission on Higher Education has also redesigned its reaccreditation process to harness continuous improvement principles and has developed an important guidebook for student learning and assessment.[6]

CONTINUOUS IMPROVEMENT VS. QUALITY ASSURANCE

Although there is undoubtedly a current convergence of interest concerning continuous improvement in higher education, there are also other discussions occurring in other settings that may sound similar but are actually addressing very different issues. There appears to be a strong interest in Great Britain regarding the topic of quality assurance, which may sound similar to continuous improvement but is actually dealing with very different issues. Whereas continuous improvement focuses on an understanding of the importance of statistical variation in work processes, the importance of group dynamics in improving work processes, and the importance of organizational dynamics in fostering change, quality assurance focuses in a very different direction. The contemporary concern about quality assurance in higher education would appear to be more about ensuring that academic programs meet a common standard rather than seeking to continuously improve. Quality assurance often appears to promote conformity to external requirements and may appear to be more about maintaining control rather than seeking excellence. Morley has offered a critique of the quality assurance effort in Great Britain as an effort by the state to gain greater control over the education system. Quality assurance, Morley asserts, is being used to "invade interior spaces, silence opposition, and promote conformity."[7] There is a significant difference between an emphasis on continuous improvement and a focus on quality assurance.

SUMMARY

There are many examples of enthusiastic efforts to start continuous improvement initiatives in all types of higher educational institutions. Those that focus only on fixing immediate problems tend to disappear when the immediate problems are resolved. Those that grow into focusing on the institution's management system are sustained because they continue to add value to the institution. Focus on the management system means using a systematic approach to strategic planning, conducting self-assessments, utilizing benchmarking methods, and developing an effective process for measurement and feedback. These systemic processes, in turn, drive the creation of many additional teams that continue to improve processes throughout the campus.

NOTES

1. Ron Coley and Paul K. Diamond, *Pursuing Excellence in Higher Education* (San Francisco: Jossey-Bass, 2004).

2. Gary Bonvillian and Terry Dennis, *TQM in Higher Education*, ed. Serbrenia J. Sims and Ronald R. Sims (Westport, CT: Praeger Publishers, 1995).

3. Lois Waters, *TQM in Higher Education*.

4. Annie Woolridge, *TQM in Higher Education*.

5. Walter Wheatley, *TQM in Higher Education*.

6. Middle States Commission on Higher Education, *Student Learning Assessment: Options and Resource*, Philadelphia, PA, 2003.

7. Louise Morley, *Quality and Power in Higher Education* (Berkshire, UK: Open University Press, 2003).

CHAPTER

Embarking on Continuous Improvements in the Academic Community

> You have to start with where you are and only you know where that is.
> —Steve Brigham, AAHE CQI Project

There is no one right way for a research university, a regional university, a four-year college, or a community college to embark on the journey for continuous improvement. Each institution starts from a unique place and deals with a unique set of personalities and historical circumstances. This book will provide guidance on a variety of components that make up a comprehensive approach to continuous quality improvement in the academic community. Different chapters may be of greater interest to various readers based on the organizational setting, campus culture, and circumstances of the reader.

The continuous improvement journey engages people in learning about their organization. Adult educators have developed a term called *praxis* to refer to the manner in which we apply theory to our real life situations and modify our theory based on our experiences, and the manner in which we modify our day-to-day practices based upon our assessment and reassessment of theory.[1] Thinking reflectively about how we manage the complex processes of higher education and research is the heart of any professional practice. The body of knowledge that constitutes continuous improvement provides a broad set of theory and tools that enhances this praxis and elevates our understanding of our institutions to new levels.

There are several ways to approach the continuous improvement body of knowledge. Although it may be tempting to just jump right in and start taking actions, actions in any system will generate unexpected results. Having a theoretical framework for continuous improvement will be helpful in anticipating and dealing with changes that result when a systematic approach to continuous improvement is initiated.

This chapter begins by looking at two frameworks for the continuous improvement body of knowledge—a planning, control, improvement model, and a different model based on left brain and right brain thinking.

THE PLANNING, CONTROL, AND IMPROVEMENT MODEL

Continuous improvement professionals often accept the idea of dividing the body of knowledge into three broad categories: planning, control, and improvement.[2]

The concept of planning in academe includes the development of strategic plans that incorporate the needs of all stakeholder groups, the use of effective planning tools to organize academic and administrative programs, and the use of data to determine programmatic needs.

Control refers to the manner in which faculty, administrators, and students receive feedback that helps them modify their performance. Student feedback regarding faculty and classes is a quality control mechanism. Academic program reviews by external accrediting organizations are another form of quality control in academia. Peer reviews control the quality of papers that are published. Examinations control the quality of graduates in academic programs. All discussions regarding the question of maintaining academic standards fall under the heading of control of academic processes.

Improvement includes the development of new academic programs to meet new needs, the development of new teaching methods and improved learning through the use of new technology, and actions that make it easier for students, faculty, and other stakeholders to receive the administrative support they need. Continuous improvement engages faculty members in improving the manner in which they work together to administer their department. When faculty members conduct focus groups and surveys with students, alumni, or external stakeholders, they are engaging in a continuous improvement process. When the library staff develops a new on-line reference service to better meet the needs of faculty and students, they are also participating in continuous improvement. Likewise, when the college's purchasing department develops a new process to make it easier for faculty to order supplies, that is also continuous improvement.

Some organizational methods, such as self-assessments and the use of teams, are effective mechanisms for planning, control, and improvement.

LEFT BRAIN AND RIGHT BRAIN MODEL

It is sometimes helpful to examine continuous improvement (the body of knowledge) from the perspective of the Nobel Prize winner Roger Sperry, who initiated the study of the relationship between the brain's right and left hemispheres.[3] Sperry, and others, have postulated that the left half of the brain tends to function by processing information in an analytical, rational, logical, sequential way. The right half of the brain may function by recognizing relationships, integrating and synthesizing information, and arriving at intuitive and creative insights. (This theory is still under debate within the scientific community, but it certainly works well for explaining why people approach continuous improvement from different perspectives.)

In other words, the left side of the brain may deal with a problem or situation by collecting data, making analyses, and using a rational thinking process to reach a conclusion. The right side of the brain may approach the same problem or situation by making intuitive leaps to answers based on insight, creativity, and perceptions. The left brain may tend to break information apart for analysis, while the right brain may tend to put information together to synthesize a whole picture.

As a body of knowledge, continuous improvement covers a broad range of concepts, tools, and techniques. Some of these concepts, tools, and techniques are clearly in the orderly, analytical "left-brain" arena, such as using statistical tools and organizing plans to ensure the quality of projects and processes. Others are in the creative and synthesizing "right-brain" arena, such as using relationship diagrams to solve problems, forming teams to analyze systems, and applying intuitive concepts, such as zero defects.

Because of this broad range of concepts and approaches, it should come as no surprise when people become engaged in spirited debates over how to improve a process. People who are more comfortable using left-brain thinking processes will be exasperated with their right-brain colleagues because they seem to lack an appreciation for the careful use of data. Right-brain thinkers might be irritated with their left-brain colleagues for being too rigid in their thinking or too slow to grasp the causes of a problem. Of course, both positions are relative to how an individual processes information. Neither is right or wrong, but each may be more effective in certain circumstances.

This dichotomy between systematic left-brain and creative right-brain approaches permeates the entire range of discussion about continuous improvement, as shown in Table 2.1. The basic definition of continuous improvement, the methods for achieving it, and the approach to solving problems all hinge on patterns of thinking and information processing.

How we each think will influence how we perceive continuous improvement. An interesting variety of tools has been created that can be useful to both the left-brain and right-brain thinker, so regardless of one's thinking style, there are some tools that will feel comfortable and obvious and others that may seem of little value, based on the way each individual will organize and process information.

It is important for educators to recognize their thinking patterns (and those of others) and to be cognizant of these patterns' strengths and weaknesses in dealing with information. A person who enjoys creative thinking may need to strive to also recognize the usefulness of systematic thinking and appreciate the need to pause and pay attention to planning

Table 2.1
Comparison of Continuous Improvement Approaches

"Left-brain" approach to CI	"Right-brain" approach to CI
Solve problems through the use of data.	Solve problems through seeing of relationships.
Perform statistical analysis of data.	Use diagrams to visually show cause and effect.
Develop solutions using logical analyses of facts.	Develop solutions using creativity and brainstorming.
Define quality as conformance to requirements that can be measured.	Define quality as a holistic concept.
Establish controls to assure quality.	View quality as a process for continuous improvement in which controls can only be temporary.
Improve quality by studying variation within existing systems.	Improve quality by starting with a holistic strategic plan.
Systematic assessment of the entire system.	Start where people feel pain.

and organizing data and systems. Systematic thinkers, on the other hand, may want to allow more creative thinking into their methodical approach.

Educators who choose to deny the validity of other thinking styles will close themselves off from their colleagues and limit their growth by avoiding different approaches to addressing different situations. When people cling to their comfortable thinking processes, they restrict themselves in the manner by which they will be able to define a problem or situation. As it is often said among quality practitioners, "If the only tool you have is a hammer, every problem looks like a nail."

THE ACADEMIC SYSTEM

Each academic institution functions as a system and will conform to the observations of systems theory. Systems are composed of subsystems that co-vary, meaning a change in one part of the system (such as a change in curriculum in the Engineering School) will impact other parts of the system (such as the Library, Admissions, the Physics Department, and so on).

Some systems are relatively open, allowing information to easily enter and leave the system, while others are closed, keeping information about the institution inside and keeping new ideas out. As a body of knowledge, continuous improvement promotes open systems and the study of co-varying processes in order to optimize the performance of the system as a whole. This is often carried out by study of a particular subsystem—such as the Student Financial Aid office—recognizing that changes will have a positive or negative affect on other parts of the system, such as the English Department.

A college or university is a complex system made up of hundreds of subsystems. Dysfunctionality in a subsystem can impact every other system on campus. Introducing continuous improvement to the academic community means introducing a set of diagnostic concepts and tools that will help subsystems improve in their performance. As each subsystem improves, the overall health of the institution likewise improves. Or, as is often said among continuous improvement practitioners, a rising tide raises all ships.

A PHASE MODEL

Continuous improvement can best be introduced to an academic community through the use of a phase model that is based on the recognition of academe's unique nature, as seen from a systems perspective. The rate at which an institution moves through these phases depends on the commitment of the leadership to provide staff resources to facilitate and teach the quality concepts.

The Formative Phase

The first phase of quality in higher education is a formative phase, in which the institution begins to explore the concept of continuous improvement. Initial information may come from studying other schools, working with local businesses or healthcare organizations, or working with an accrediting association.

The formative phase may include initial seminars and workshops that help people develop their use of diagnostic tools. Initial opportunities for improving subsystems are identified and work groups or teams begin to gain experience at analyzing and improving the performance of a system. The institution may begin to conduct some initial fact-finding and self-discovery in terms of who its stakeholders are and what they think about the institution. There may be some urgent problems that need to be solved or subsystems that have an urgent need for the development of a strategic plan. These cannot be ignored, so the formative phase often involves the formation of teams to work on systems in urgent need of improvement.

During the first phase, the organization needs to begin to develop the concept of a management system. This may start with some reflection on what system is really currently in use to manage the institution. What data does the leadership use in decision making at each level of the institution? Who are the stakeholders the institution serves, and how do we know what their needs are and if we are meeting their needs? These are systemic issues that must be addressed over time. The institution must find a balance in working on immediate problems and in reflecting on and improving the overall management system.

It is a good idea in the formative phase to seek outside perspectives and advice on how to proceed. Several schools have started by sending teams to visit other colleges to observe their continuous improvement activities firsthand and to talk directly with faculty and administrators. It is useful to bring in speakers from other colleges and universities who can share their experiences from their campuses. When Belmont University launched its continuous improvement initiative, it drew upon the experiences of Samford University. Villanova drew upon the experiences at Penn State. Berkeley visited six campuses and adopted effective practices from several. Alabama studied Penn State and the University of Wisconsin–Madison, while Binghamton studied Villanova and Rutgers. The University of Central Oklahoma and the Miami University of Ohio have studied Alabama.

It is also useful to draw upon the knowledge and experience of corporations that are interested in furthering the use of the quality in higher education. The University of Wisconsin–Madison drew on the experiences of IBM and Proctor and Gamble in starting its quality initiative. Rutgers has gained many insights from Johnson and Johnson. Purdue has a retired director of quality from Motorola on its Excellence 21 Steering Committee. Alabama established a Quality Advisory Board (QAB) for the president and executive staff of the institution that consists of representatives of companies that have all won the Malcolm Baldrige National Quality Award. This includes a manager from Milliken, a quality professional from Federal Express, a Boeing fellow, and a quality manager from the Ritz-Carlton Hotels. Corporate leaders in quality are very willing to advise higher educational institutions in their efforts for continuous improvement. Alabama's QAB meets twice a year with the president and executive staff to discuss the progress in using continuous improvement.

It is wise to begin to consider how to engage the faculty in the formative phase of the CI initiative. Faculty involvement first comes in the areas where the faculty is experiencing pain and needs some outside, neutral facilitation. This can be in the form of assistance in developing a strategic plan for an academic unit or in helping an academic unit resolve an immediate problem. At the University of Wisconsin–Madison, one of the early quality initiatives involved the Department of Zoology, where the department chair Dr. Warren Porter applied quality methods to improving faculty meetings, developed a departmental strategic plan, improved fund-raising, and developed a culture of collaboration among the faculty.[4] Belmont University engaged faculty in a Liberal Studies Education Team to "rethink" the school's general education requirement.[5]

It is also advisable to enlist the support of faculty members who teach disciplines that are familiar with continuous improvement concepts, such as industrial engineering and business administration.

These early activities are the baby steps in introducing CI concepts. Success speeds success in this type of change process. Although only a small number of people may initially buy in to the quality concepts at first, their success will convince the majority of people on campus who will take a wait-and-see perspective.

It is equally important to plan to involve academic administrators and administrators of support programs in the quality improvement initiative. The institution can create a council that will involve deans, department chairs, and administrators in support functions in organizing and guiding the quality initiative. A core of champions among these administrators will provide the early success stories that will help other administrators see the value of continuous improvement.

An effective exercise in the formative phase is to ask the question, "What would we do if we wanted to make sure this initiative will fail?" On most campuses, people can readily answer this question. Their answers then serve as important markers concerning the types of actions that will need to be taken in order to have a successful continuous improvement initiative.

The Growth Phase

Within a couple of years, the quality activities can expand into a growth phase. During this phase, the level of seminars and workshops will remain fairly high. The organization is working to introduce many people to a wide set of tools and concepts.

The growth phase is where the organization begins to reap the benefits of having trained work groups in the quality tools and from training people across the organization in using facilitation skills. Academic and staff groups are using the quality concepts and tools that meet their specific needs, often without the need for help from anyone else.

The level of project activity goes up, often so fast that no one can really keep track of everything that is going on. Staff groups all across the campus are using the quality tools and concepts to a point where they are starting to seem normal to everyone. Managers are establishing cross-functional teams as the normal way to address problems that used to be ignored.

The external boundaries of the system continue to open up. Academic and staff groups begin to engage in benchmarking. Within the context of higher education, benchmarking often means comparing a school's performance with similar institutions to ensure that the institution is similar to its peers. Within the context of continuous improvement, benchmarking means identifying an issue on campus that needs improvement, identifying another institution that has developed one of the best approaches to dealing with this particular issue, studying what that institution has done, and adopting that institution's practices. Faculty is interested in finding out how other academic units at other institutions are handling problems and achieving results. Staff groups are "honorably adopting" better ideas from other institutions and other parts of the campus.

Internally, academic and staff managers are not afraid to own up to having a problem and seeking some external help to resolve the issue.

Deans are more likely to seek a neutral person to facilitate their strategic planning activities. Administrators sense that it is safe to admit that some processes are not working well and are relieved to be able to get some help in diagnosing the problem.

In the growth phase, the organization begins to develop the structure of its management system. Stakeholder groups are clearly identified and data regarding their needs and satisfaction begins to be assembled. Organizations may take their existing data collection processes more seriously. Many organizations will initiate new stakeholder satisfaction surveys and will use this data to identify problems and to give feedback to the staff and faculty. Administrators will begin to look more seriously at obtaining comparative data with other institutions and will study the performance trends from their own data.

As part of the development of the management system, the organization will begin to look at strategic planning from a broader, more systematic perspective. There may be greater willingness for academic and staff units to collaborate in the development of strategic plans.

The institution can begin to tell its stakeholders about the early results of using the CI concepts during the growth phase. Improvements can be publicized in the campus newspaper. A newsletter or quality Web site can be established to provide information on teams and access to quality tools and information on the World Wide Web, guiding faculty and staff to resources and information on who to contact for help. In this phase, the institution can begin to give feedback to parents, alumni, and students regarding the results of surveys and actions being taken. The faculty should receive a report of activities, along with the student government. Recognition should be given to departments, staff, and cross-functional teams and task forces that work on improving processes.

The Mature Phase

Even highly successful organizations that have won the Malcolm Baldrige National Quality Award find that quality is a journey and that no organization ever fully arrives. There is always more that can and should be done. Entering into a mature phase does not mean resting on one's laurels but instead requires holding onto the gains that have already been met, living up to a reputation for quality, and finding even better ways to delight the stakeholders.

An organization in the mature phase will continue its commitment to learning by offering a wide range of workshops and seminars that develop facilitative leadership skills among academic and support program administrators. There will always be a turnover in administrative positions, student government leaders, and faculty leadership, so there will always be a need to develop new leaders.

In a mature phase, the institution has a large number of people who are adept at diagnosing problems, designing methods to collect data, and in using data to make decisions. Problems are routinely solved by involving the people who do the work in diagnosing the problem. There is no reluctance to organize a team to go after a potential improvement. Work processes have been flowcharted and measurements are in place.

Institutions in the mature phase have gained some experiences using self-assessment criteria based on a Baldrige model (see Chapter 4) and compare themselves against this high standard in order to identify greater opportunities for continuous improvement.

Strategic planning is an ongoing process all across the campus in the mature phase. While each organization may be in a somewhat different stage in its strategic planning process, all organizational units have a planning cycle, and all are linked to an overall plan for the institution.

An agreed-upon management system is defined and in use during the mature phase. A new dean or department chair can receive a diagram that illustrates how his or her college or department functions. Each college has a clearly defined set of process measures and output measures that are understood by all the stakeholders. The institution continues to collect stakeholder data through surveys and focus groups, and the institutions track the data over time and observe trends in feedback.

Most members of the faculty have accepted the CI body of knowledge as a legitimate perspective for improving the institution and feel that the CI movement has made their jobs better in the mature phase. Most members of the faculty should be able to point to a work process that now provides them better service or should be able to identify an activity where the quality process helped their department establish a strategic plan. In the mature phase, faculty members explore ways to apply the continuous improvement tools and concepts to the manner in which they teach and conduct their research.

Institutions in the mature phase are publishing the results of their efforts and taking a leadership role in educating other campuses in their geographic region or among their institutional peers about continuous improvement methods.

A CONTINUOUS IMPROVEMENT COUNCIL

One of the improvement gurus, Dr. Joseph Juran, developed the idea of establishing a council within an organization to drive the continuous implementation process. Purdue, Villanova, and Penn State have all made effective use of the CI council concept.

The University Council of Continuous Quality Improvement at Pennsylvania State University is chaired by the provost. It is important for the provost to lead the council for many reasons. First, the provost typically has most of the institution reporting to her or him and has significant influence to encourage organizations to get involved with continuous improvement. Second, the continuous improvement initiative must be linked to the academic units from the beginning. If it is viewed as an activity designed just for improving the administrative support groups, such as maintenance, parking, and student services, it may not be embraced by the entire institution. Third, the provost is a pivotal player in the development of the institution's strategy and can ensure that continuous improvement and strategic planning are fully integrated.

Purdue's Excellence 21 steering committee is chaired by their coordinator, Kathy Newton (who is also a member of the faculty), but includes members from Academic Affairs, Business Services, University Relations, Intercollegiate Athletics, and deans and directors from various academic units.

The CI Council is an excellent mechanism for bringing key members of the academic community into closer contact with the quality initiative. The council may include deans, faculty, students, and administrators from student affairs, financial affairs, intercollegiate athletics, and other support groups. A council can be designed so that members serve for a year and then allow new members to rotate onto the council. In this way, all the deans can serve on the council within a few years. At The University of Alabama, the faculty representatives are selected by the Faculty Senate, while the student representatives are selected by the Student Government Association. Administrators from support groups rotate onto the council to provide the broadest exposure possible to quality concepts across the campus.

The function of the CI Council will evolve as the institution moves through the phase model. In the formative phase, the council will attend and critique training workshops, advise on external speakers, and champion early initiatives. In the growth phase, the council will begin the discussion of systemic issues and the development of a management system. During this phase, the council may lead the institution in conducting a self-assessment, using a state-level quality award. In this phase, the CI Council assesses how far the institution has come and how far it needs to go. The role of the CI Council in the mature phase is to ensure that the institution can hold onto the gains it has made, to lead in the process of reassessing the institution's progress, and to ensure that the institution continues to celebrate the progress being made.

AN OFFICE OF CONTINOUS IMPROVEMENT

The location of the continuous improvement staff, both organizationally and physically, is an important issue. On many campuses, the CI function reports to the vice president for administration, who oversees financial, maintenance, and other service functions. This organizational location provides immediate access to many administrative processes that may be in need of improvement. However, this may reinforce the stereotype of continuous improvement being a business activity, unsuited for the academic community.

The CI staff on several campuses, such as Penn State and the University of Wisconsin–Madison, reports to the provost or vice president for academic affairs. This gives access to all the academic units and encourages academic department chairs and deans to participate in seminars that provide skills in participative leadership that fit well into the academic culture. At Berkeley, the continuous improvement office reports to the chancellor's office. At Rutgers University and Purdue University, the continuous improvement leader also serves as a tenured member of the faculty.

The physical location of the CI staff can also be important, because office location is sometimes a barometer of administrative support for programs in the campus culture. The president of The University of Alabama chose to place the Office of Continuous Quality Improvement between the president's and the provost's offices as a symbol of the significance of the continuous improvement initiative.

In other cases, a campus may want to emphasize the role of the CI staff as a neutral party that will fairly address the concerns of faculty, administration, and students. The office may be symbolically located in an area that focuses on ease of access and room for discussions and teams to work. Binghamton University organized a Center for Quality that focuses on facilitating projects for campus organizations. The center helps organizations describe their issues, plan meetings or retreats, and facilitate meetings to help keep groups on track with problem solving and process redesign.

Regardless of the reporting relationship and location of an office, the continuous improvement staff must work actively with the CI Council, if the campus elects to have a council, and should support the Council's chairperson in planning and organizing its meetings. If the institution develops an advisory board of external advisors, the continuous improvement staff should be the group on campus that recruits the board members, organizes meetings, and keeps them up to speed with activities on the campus.

Campuses have a variety of names for their continuous improvement organizations, as well as a variety of locations and reporting relationships. Both Penn State and the University of Wisconsin–Madison link their continuous improvement functions with institutional strategic planning. On some campuses, the quality staff functions from an organizational development perspective. Binghamton University has four staff members in its Center for Quality, which handles a large amount of team facilitation. Southwest Texas State University has an associate vice president for quality and planning. Purdue University Calumet has an assistant vice chancellor for academic quality, while Villanova has the Villanova Quality Initiative Office.

It must also be noted that many campuses are making significant progress on continuous improvement initiatives that are primarily focused in administrative areas. The University of Miami's continuous improvement initiative has established itself as a national leader in developing performance measures in administrative programs. The California State University System has an impressive initiative that concentrates in administrative services. Berkeley's balanced scorecard system in their Business and Administrative Services is receiving interest from across the country.

THREE DIMENSIONS OF CONTINUOUS IMPROVEMENT

Continuous improvement initiatives engage the academic community in three dimensions: the macrodimension that examines how the institution operates, the microdimension that considers how specific processes function, and the public dimension that involves the manner in which its external stakeholders perceive higher education.

Most administrators can readily accept the benefits that a continuous improvement initiative provides at the micro level. CI endeavors at campuses across the country have yielded a mountain of examples of improvement in specific processes. The National Consortium for Continuous Improvement in Higher Education conducts annual conferences where universities share numerous examples of specific process improvements. This book will likewise provide a multitude of examples of process improvements that have resulted from CI activities at a variety of colleges and universities.

Micro-level improvements are essential for many reasons. First, process improvements mean better services for students and faculty, making the campus more appealing and less stressful. In many cases, specific process improvements also lead to reduced costs and improvements in efficiency of operations in terms of improved student recruiting, academic performance, and retention.

Occasional, random improvements do not significantly alter an institution. However, a systemic, aggressive drive for improvement will create hundreds of specific improvements that will have a profound, pervasive effect on the institution. Creating a culture of continuous improvement can transform the manner in which a campus operates and can significantly change the way that students, faculty, and other stakeholders view their institution.

On the macro level, the quality discipline enables institutional leaders to compare their performance against a common yardstick, such as the Malcolm Baldrige National Quality Award. Continuous improvement not only focuses on improvement of specific processes but causes the organization to reassess the manner in which it establishes and uses measures of institutional performance and the manner in which it conducts strategic planning. In some parts of the country, continuous improvement is emerging as a better way to evaluate and reaccredit colleges and universities.

A continuous improvement initiative eventually affects the public dimension of an institution. When an institution of higher education pursues a state or national quality award, people notice. Trustees from corporations understand the significance of the Baldrige Award as a yardstick for excellence. Corporations responded to the University of Wisconsin–Stout's winning of the Baldrige Award with a 50 percent increase in the number of visits to interview their graduates. As institutions seek to differentiate themselves from competing public and private campuses, evidence of excellence will increasingly be derived from comparison against defined criteria, such as regional and national quality awards.

CREATING A MANAGEMENT SYSTEM

Many institutions can claim that they conduct strategic planning. Few can document how their strategic planning process is actually conducted in a systematic manner or cite examples as to how the process is studied and improved. This is the distinction between an institution that has a management system and the institution that is simply responding to situations, taking actions without a systematic approach that is articulated and understood by everyone on the campus.

Few institutions have done a better job of designing, understanding, and improving their management system than the University of Wisconsin–Stout. Located in Menomonie, Wisconsin, the Stout campus has developed a well-documented methodology for managing the campus that includes a systematic approach to strategic planning, a well-defined budgeting process that involves the whole campus, and clearly defined processes for managing academic programs and administrative support areas.

Stout has pioneered the consistent use of a program director model for managing their academic programs. While the school continues to have deans and department chairs who manage departmental staffing and budgets and schedule classes, each academic program has a faculty member who serves as a program director who oversees the horizontal flow of the academic program. The program director works with advisory committees to develop and update curriculum, manages student recruitment and advising, and coordinates contact with employers and professional organizations to bring their perspectives into the curriculum and to enable graduating students to connect with employers. The program director is also a key participant in the review of a program for reaccreditation. Program directors serve as the advocates for their programs and can address concerns about the performance of any department in meeting the students' needs in their program.

University of Wisconsin–Stout has also adopted a systematic approach for designing and implementing new academic programs. New programs are based on evidence that there is a need for the program based on state, regional, and national information. Student demand and future enrollment are systematically assessed, along with options for designing a new program in collaboration with another institution. Curriculum and methods of program assessment are defined, faculty requirements are established, library resources and facility needs are understood, and an operating budget is prepared before the new program gets underway. Many other institutions may actually follow these steps, but few have a procedure that defines the process, along with forms that are systematically used to organize and assess the information.

Although Stout's approach to strategic planning, campus governance, budgeting, academic program management, and extensive use of surveys and focus groups and performance measures that generate data for decision making may not be absolutely unique, the combination of these CI methods in a clearly documented and well-understood system exemplifies the concept of a management system and has earned them the Malcolm Baldrige National Quality Award.

A comprehensive management system integrates planning, control, and improvement in a clearly articulated and systematic manner. There are many visual models for illustrating a management system. One model for a continuous improvement management system emphasizes a continuous cycle of assessment, planning, implementation of change, and performance (see Figure 2.1).

Subsequent chapters will build on this concept of a cycle of improvement. Chapter 4 will examine options for assessment and Chapter 5 will examine planning for academic and administrative programs.

This model can be applied to a specific class, a curriculum, the operation of an academic or administrative office, an academic department, an entire college, or even a university.

SUMMARY

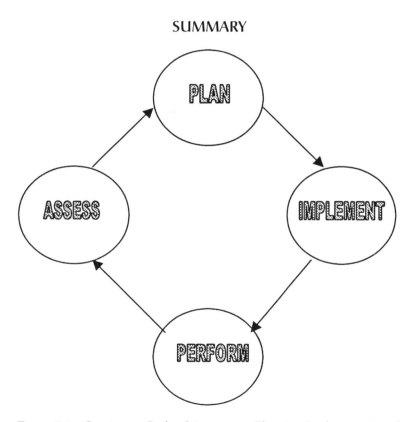

Figure 2.1   Continuous Cycle of Assessment, Planning, Implementation of Change, and Performance

The commitment to continuous improvement is a long-term investment in any institutional setting. Institutions will move at different speeds through the start-up and growth phases of continuous improvement, depending on their culture and the approach that best fits their environment. There is no single best way to implement continuous improvement, but the phases are fairly predictable. In most cases, it is essential to have concurrent movement on the analysis and improvement of the management system while also achieving early successes in solving more immediate institutional problems.

NOTES

1. Paulo Freire, *The Politics of Education* (South Hadley, MA: Bergin & Garvey, 1981).

2. Joseph Juran, *Juran on Leadership for Quality* (New York: Macmillan, 1989).

3. Roger Sperry, *Science and Moral Priority* (New York: Columbia University Press, 1983).

4. Warren P. Porter and Kathleen A. Paris, "Creating a Strategic Plan," Department of Zoology, The University of Wisconsin–Madison, 1998.

5. The Conference Board, "Quality Profile: Belmont University," July 1997.

CHAPTER 3

Educating the Campus about Continuous Improvement

Struggle is a part of it; there is no "best" way.
—Susan Williams, Belmont University

Educating the campus about continuous improvement is a complicated challenge. There are a wide range of concepts and tools that will be appropriate for different campus settings. Most campuses comprise many different academic and administrative groups that will have different needs and opportunities for different types of improvement tools and concepts. Any effort to make a "forced march" by sending large numbers of people through a single set of improvement workshops will probably generate more resistance than value.

For long-term improvement in higher education, it is important to design a continuous improvement initiative that is both "bottom-up" and "top-down." Organizations need the "bottom-up" activities, where work groups engage in diagnosis and improvement of their work processes, engage in strategic planning for their work unit, and experience personal empowerment in shaping the destiny of their organization. At the same time, it is important for the institution to look at improvement from a "top-down" perspective through comprehensive strategic planning, critical examination and improvement of management systems, and by using data to make decisions that guide the institution.

While acknowledging the idiosyncratic nature of most campuses, the fact remains that certain quality concepts and tools will be very useful in a wide range of settings at higher educational institutions. It is important to introduce most campus organizations to the concepts of variation and of work flow, and the understanding of the principle of the vital few. These are basic quality principles that should be understood by everyone at all levels of the academic community. If an organization overlooks these basic principles, it may become mired in counterproductive activities.

UNDERSTANDING VARIATION

Colleges and universities encounter all manner of variation in academic and administrative processes but may not recognize the nature of the variation or the importance of the variation in understanding how a system functions. Often, the tendency is to react too quickly to variation without understanding it, thereby making situations worse.

In some cases, institutions are rather fickle about how they discuss data. When numbers look good, they trumpet it in publications. When numbers do not look good, they are ignored. This leads people to focus on individual data points rather than on trends.

For example, most universities recruit international students from dozens of countries. In one year, an institution may have 398 international students. The next year the number may jump to 430, and people applaud the "progress." The third year has 382 international students, and people look for reasons to blame for the drop. The fourth year brings in 412 students, and everyone is satisfied that the institution is now on the right track. In year five, the number is 428, and it is mentioned in every publication to highlight the success. In year six, the international student enrollment falls to 401, and people wonder if a new person needs to be hired to manage the office.

When we look at the individual data points for each year and only compare it as an increase or decrease from the previous year, we create an illusion with the data. To better understand what is actually happening, we need to display the data longitudinally, using a run chart. Figure 3.1 charts the data points from the international student example and connects them by a line.

If we add up the six data points and divide by the number of data points (2451 divided by 6), we will find that the average international student enrollment is 408 over the six-year period. In Figure 3.2, we add the average value to our run chart as a line that denotes 408 as a central tendency.

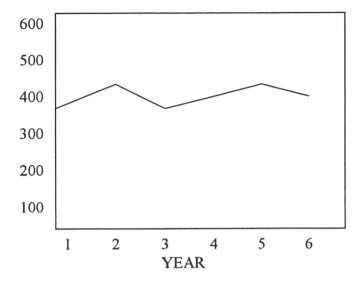

Figure 3.1   International Student Enrollment

From this perspective, we can see that the international student enrollment process is very stable and predictable. Unless a significant change occurs, each year we can predict enrollment at 408, plus or minus about 20.

There is variation in this system from year to year, but the variation is built into the system, or common to it. Statisticians will refer to this type of variation as "common cause variation."[1]

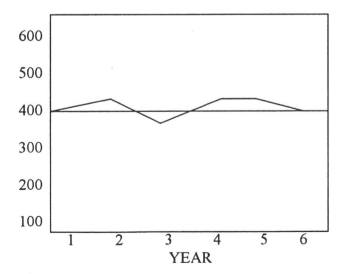

Figure 3.2   International Student Enrollment

Realizing that the international student enrollment process is stable, subject to common cause variation, is very useful and raises several questions. One question would be to ask how we know the extent of variation we might expect to see in a stable system. That question can be answered by calculating the range of variation that is three standard deviations above and below the central tendency. Statisticians have derived a variety of calculations to determine the statistical "control limits" for various types of data that enable people to determine when the variation in a system is due to common causes and when the system has been influenced by a "special cause" of variation.

In the case of this example, we would expect most of the data points for student enrollment to fall within one standard deviation of the central tendency, but we would not be surprised if occasionally we saw enrollment approaching three standard deviations.

If we repeatedly saw data close to or beyond three standard deviations, we would know that the system has experienced some special cause of variation. For example, a sudden change in national policy regarding student visas could generate a significant decrease or increase in international student enrollment. Someone has changed the system.

Suppose the strategic plan of the institution calls for increasing international student enrollment to over 600 within the next three years. This will not happen by fiat, nor will encouragement to "try harder" make much difference. The system is stable, yielding 408 plus or minus twenty students each year. To increase the enrollment, we must change the system.

Changing the system is both a scientific and political process. The political process involves assembling the right group of people to study and modify the process, giving their efforts legitimacy on the campus and providing them time to work and access the necessary data.

The scientific process involves the accurate description of the current process (usually using a flowchart), the collection of data regarding the performance of the process, and the development of theories as to how the process can be changed to achieve the desired increase in enrollment. The team may need to benchmark other institutions, conduct focus groups with international students, survey international alumni, or use other methods to collect and analyze data to develop a thorough understanding of how the process currently functions and how it can be improved.

Once changes are planned, a new flowchart should be created to define the redesigned system. When changes are implemented, data should be collected to determine how the new system is performing, and the team should continue to study the process to ensure it is now yielding the necessary results.

Consider the risks to the campus if actions are taken without understanding whether the variation in a system is "in control"—meaning it is subject to common cause variation that is built into the system—or "out of control"—meaning it is subject to special causes of variation that are outside of the system. What if the institution replaced recruiters based on a decrease of forty students? This stable system is guaranteed to see drops of forty, so recruiters would be guaranteed of being fired, regardless of their performance, if they were willing to stay.

Most academic and administrative organizations on campus have at least a few places where they would benefit from collecting data into run charts. Organizing data into run charts, showing the central tendency of the data, and asking a statistics professor to calculate the control limits is a powerful way for understanding whether a process is stable.

THE CONCEPT OF WORK FLOW

All work on college and university campuses is a process, whether ordering books for the library, conducting a research project, or designing a course curriculum. All processes can be charted, analyzed, and improved. Faculty members who specialize in education and learning recognize that teaching is also a process, even though their peers who teach may not recognize this fact.

Academic and administrative processes can be described using the Input-Process-Output Model. The final quality of the output depends on the quality of the inputs and the quality of the transformational process. For example, consider the process of recruiting and enrolling freshmen.

Input	Process	Output
High School Seniors	Contact with High Schools	College Freshmen
	Developing recruitment materials	
	Distribution of recruitment materials	
	Campus Visits	
	Application Review Process	
	Student/Parent Orientation	
	Scholarship Review/Awards	

Institutions want to recruit the best possible students. Problems would arise if the high schools in a region failed to prepare students for college-level work. If there are quality problems with the inputs into any process, those problems either require extra effort to counteract or overcome the problem, or the problem will be passed through to the output stage.

Other problems would arise if any of the work processes were ineffective. For instance, if the scholarship process is slow and cumbersome, good students may select other schools, because they did not hear about possible scholarships in a timely manner. If campus visits were poorly organized, students and parents would be turned off by their visit. If there were problems with contacting high schools, then many potential students might never hear about the institution. Quality of outputs, or results, hinges on quality of inputs and the quality of work processes.

The quality of academic processes can also be visualized with an Input-Process-Output model, as in this example of teaching an introductory music class, where the goal is to enable students to distinguish between styles of classical music.

Input	Process	Output
Students	Classroom presentations	Student has gained an
Professor	Provide music examples	ability to distinguish
Recordings	Written Tests	between types of
Classroom	Review of the materials the students did not recognize.	classical music.
	Students study.	

If there are problems with the inputs, such as a classroom with noisy distractions, the quality of the learning will be diminished. If there are problems with the learning process, such as a poorly prepared explanation of baroque music or a CD player that does not work, then the quality of the "output" will be diminished.

Academic institutions are a massive assembly of processes. The core processes deal with learning, which can be categorized into a variety of types of processes. The faculty members are responsible for the core processes and are expected to have demonstrated expertise in their subject field. Academic institutions go to significant lengths to ensure that faculty members have subject matter expertise through review of credentials, promotion, and tenure reviews. The overall quality of core academic processes is the subject of curriculum reviews and academic program reviews. The general public has little appreciation for the degree of rigor built into the academic system to ensure the quality and productivity of the faculty. Many faculty members are also critically aware of the processes they use to engage their students in learning. Some, however, simply mimic the process they experienced as a student, without understanding the learning theory that is relevant to their discipline. In order to provide faculty members with feedback about the effectiveness of their teaching process, most institutions have implemented some form of student feedback regarding classes. Student performance on examinations is also valuable data to determine the effectiveness of the learning process, subject to variations in both the inputs (quality of students) and the process.

Learning processes are particularly challenging because the outcome depends not only on the efforts of the institution and faculty to create the right setting for learning, but also depends on the effort and capabilities of the students. Student performance is influenced by the students' social life and the amount and type of nonacademic work they must perform in order to afford an education. This complexity makes it easy for faculty to blame students for poor performance, even if there is significant opportunity for improving how a course is taught or how an overall curriculum fits together.

Surrounding the core academic processes are hundreds of administrative processes to support the needs of students, faculty, and all those who provide support services to the campus community.

For better or worse, academic institutions exist within a changing world. Communication systems grow, new industries emerge, and demographics change over time. All processes must be open to on-going study and analysis for continuous improvement or else they become static, stale, and eventually out of step with the people they were created to serve. When an academic or administrative process is not critiqued, it becomes rigid and may be ineffective.

It is useful in almost any academic and administrative setting to engage people in visually defining, or mapping, the flow of their work processes. Two similar approaches can be used. The concept was introduced at Alabama as Flowcharting and at Binghamton as Process Mapping.

FLOWCHARTING

Flowcharting is a powerful way to analyze and discuss a work process. There are many reasons to flowchart a process. First, charting the process documents and clarifies the current process. There may not be much agreement regarding how the process is currently performed. Different recruiters may have different ways they deal with prospective students. Different residence halls may develop different ways to orient students.

Flowcharts allow us to visually define how a work process is performed, showing the steps in their proper sequence. Boxes are used to indicate steps where work is done, and diamonds are used to indicate where decisions are made. Lines are used to connect the boxes, and arrows show the flow of information and sequence of actions.

Flowcharts help people talk about their work process and provide a visual point of reference that greatly enhances the discussion and analysis of a work process. Drawing the work process in a chart often creates valuable discussion and the discovery that people do not share the same understanding about how their work fits together. The flowchart helps people visually recognize the points where rework occurs and where a loop may exist, where information goes around several times before going on to the next step. The flowchart helps people decide what types of data would be useful to gather for evaluating and improving the process.

Developing a visual description of a process by using a flowchart allows people to identify bottlenecks, or constraints, in the process. For example, staff in the enrollment office at The University of Alabama felt that with new technology available, they needed to redesign their process for reviewing, approving, or rejecting student applications. A team developed a flowchart to define the current "as is" process. The team looked for bottlenecks, or constraints, in the process where an application could get sidetracked or delayed. The university can receive 10,000 applications in a three-month period, so it is important for the process to flow smoothly.

By developing a flowchart, the staff identified several areas where work could be performed differently to provide applicants with faster feedback. Flowcharts are particularly effective for speeding up a process (reducing the process cycle time). Cycle time reduction can be useful in many ways, such as providing more timely services to faculty, faster procurement of supplies, faster reimbursement for travel expenses, faster preparation of manuscripts for publication, and less time spent in meetings. The point is to improve quality, reduce rework, and make processes flow more smoothly. Flowcharting benefits the people who do the work by reducing rework and frustration, not by making them work faster.

Flowcharts can be used to quickly train new employees or student assistants in how to reliably and effectively perform a task. Flowcharts can also be used to depict the sequence of course requirements for an academic program, providing advisors and students with a visual tool to more effectively communicate and plan a student's schedule.

Flowcharting work processes is a standard part of the improvement model at Wisconsin–Madison and at Penn State. University Testing Services at Penn State, for example, formed a team to decrease the error rate in administrative handling of test forms. As part of their diagnostic process, the team prepared a flowchart of the existing process and collected data on error rates in order to develop ideas for improving the process.[2]

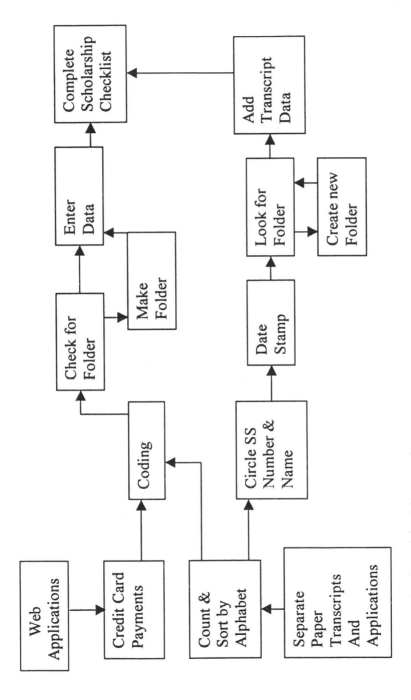

Figure 3.3 Flowchart of the Admissions Process

Villanova has made extensive use of flowcharting to improve a wide variety of campus processes. Facilities Management has used flowcharts to diagnose and improve core work processes. Flowcharts have been used in academic support groups to expedite the movement of information and forms through offices.[3]

Samford University used flowcharting as a primary tool in its continuous improvement process, using flowcharts to analyze its application process, admissions, and the core courses and examination process for their nursing students.[4] A Samford team organized an analysis of student test scores on the NLN exam in Anatomy and Physiology courses to determine reasons for poor student performance. They started with a flowchart of the examination process and then identified key performance measures. After collecting data on the performance measures, the Samford team focused on four major reasons for poor student performance and took corrective actions. The primary cause was students waiting several months after completing the Anatomy and Physiology courses before taking the NLN exam.

PROCESS MAPPING

The purpose of process mapping is to help teams identify which people and offices are involved in a specified process and to understand how they relate to each other. In working with teams, it is important to define the process that will be mapped (with a clear start and end point), to get the team to agree on what happens the majority of the time (not focusing on the exceptions), and to map recent tasks rather than abstract processes. The steps in process mapping are:

1. Clearly identify where the process will start;
2. Begin by brainstorming a list of the offices or positions involved in the process. Write each on a separate Post-It note;
3. Ask the team if any offices or persons can be combined;
4. Place the Post-Its on the left side of a large page (or slick board) in the chronological order necessary to complete the process;
5. Continue to ask the team "What happens next?" placing the responses on Post-Its and placing these horizontally across the paper. Each step must move forward across the page, no looping back;
6. Once the team has reached the end of the process, go back to the beginning and have the team walk the facilitator through the process as the facilitator draws in connecting lines. Remember to only guide the team.

The process map can be enhanced in a number of ways:

1. Number each step;

2. Create a "Why" or "Justification" page. Ask why that office or position does each step. Remind the team that the question is related to the process, not to them as an individual;

3. Brainstorm the strengths and the areas for improvement of the current process;

4. Group the strengths and areas of improvement into major categories;

5. Use Nominal Group Technique to choose the top 1, 2, or 3 categories in strengths and areas for improvement. The team should attempt to address the major areas for improvement and retain the major strengths as they design a new process;

6. Brainstorm a list of any existing policies or "hands-off" areas that the team needs to consider. Determine if these are flexible or not.

Sometimes the attempt to create a process map reveals that there is no existing process. It may be a good idea to compliment the team members on how well they have been handling the process without a formalized plan or approach and then move forward to create an official process. Employees sometimes make things work through sheer good will and determination, but creating a process map will help people agree on how the process should work. Process maps also help people understand how others are involved in the process and will be useful to cross-train and train new employees in the future.

The California State University System uses process mapping methods in numerous administrative functions to identify the suppliers and inputs, and customers and outputs of administrative processes. CSU staff have developed process maps for parking services, the student health center, enrollment services, the student union building, libraries, work order processing, accounts payable, procurement, and the career center.[5]

The Cal State System organizes process mapping workshops for people from multiple campuses. People are brought together from several campuses to map a common process, such as student accounts receivable. Other processing mapping teams are from a specific campus, such as the San Diego campus's study of its work order process.[6]

The objective of process mapping, as well as flowcharting, is to help people be critically aware of how their work processes actually flow. In some cases, the existing process may already be the best it can be. Even in these cases, the communication around and about the process can often be improved. The objective is not to burden the organization with rigid processes but to optimize the flow of work in order to provide the best possible service to students, faculty, researchers, parents, and other important stakeholders.

THE VITAL FEW

Universities invest many resources in recruiting the best possible students. Although some students will not apply themselves to their studies, most students seem to desire to successfully complete their course of studies and to graduate. If an institution has sufficient admission standards, it is reasonable to expect that all who are admitted and enrolled should be able to graduate if they are diligent in their studies, although not all will graduate in their original chosen field of study.

It does not make a great deal of sense for an institution to spend resources recruiting students that it expects to fail. If students who have the potential to succeed are not being successful, it is in the institution's interest to determine whether the students' lack of success is due to poor study habits, extracurricular activities, or problems with an academic process. The institution can and should take actions in all three areas.

The University of Alabama formed a team that included academic and student affairs staff to analyze student performance during the freshman year. Data from courses that freshmen take were analyzed to determine if there were specific courses that might account for freshmen being unsuccessful in their academic pursuits.

The team worked on the basis of the principle of the vital few, also called the Pareto principle. Vilfredo Pareto, the distinguished Italian economist, conducted research into the natural distribution of wealth in a society. Pareto found that, without artificial controls, most wealth will end up in the hands of a few, and most people end up with little wealth. The vital few are the small number that accounts for most of the important behaviors in a system. It is a few people, for example, who account for most of the absenteeism in any organization. In any system, it is wise to discover if there is some vital few that accounts for much of the behaviors or activities in that system.

The quality teacher Joseph Juran coined the term "Pareto principle" to indicate the importance of finding the vital few causes in any setting and to focus attention there first to seek for ways to change the system.[7]

So, the team studying freshmen classroom performance found that one class accounted for most of the failing grades among freshmen and that class was Freshman Math. Freshman Math actually covers math skills that high school students are expected to have mastered. However, many high school students do not seem to retain their knowledge of math, or barely get by, and are confronted with an old nemesis in this class. The vital few was now identified.

BENCHMARKING

The team working on improving freshman academic performance decided to conduct a benchmarking study regarding Freshman Math. Up to half the students who were taking the course might fail in a given semester. Someone, somewhere, must have found a more effective way to teach this material, the team reasoned. The team asked among their colleagues and heard about an intriguing project at Virginia Tech, called the Math Emporium, which used a Web-based method to teach freshman math skills. A small group went to Virginia Tech to observe the Math Emporium during the spring and were impressed by the results they saw. The team proposed the development of a large computer lab for Freshman Math. During the summer, the Math faculty members fully deployed their Math Lab and in the fall, all Freshman Math students took the course in the new Math Lab. Students could come to the Math Lab at any time from early morning to late evening to take the course. The number of students using the lab each hour was tracked and posted to enable students to select the best time for them to attend the class. Although the instruction is on-line, students can obtain further help from a cadre of tutors who are available in the lab.

Student success in the lab improved dramatically. When surveyed, students did not express delight concerning the course, because it was still a math class. However, they expressed significantly less dissatisfaction than they had with their former classes that were led by instructors. The instructors were also pleased to give up the burden of teaching these courses, which are not the most exciting classes for Math faculty to teach.

The success of the Math Lab led to further funding for a major relocation and expansion that enabled faculty members to offer other courses on-line. The Math faculty members are working to share the Web-based math classes with Alabama's high schools in order to improve student learning at the high school level. The success of the Math Lab has encouraged other faculty members to consider other opportunities where computer-based learning would be advantageous to students.

Freshman retention rates at The University of Alabama have improved for a variety of reasons. One of the critical few has been the analysis and benchmarking that resulted in the Math Lab.

SELF-ASSESSMENT, STRATEGIC PLANNING, AND THE VITAL FEW

One major objective for conducting a campus self-assessment process and a strategic planning process is to identify the vital few issues on which the institution needs to focus for improvement.

The AQIP process encourages a campus to focus its efforts on improvements in a few specific areas. Likewise, the Southern Association for Colleges and Schools' new quality initiative encourages schools to identify a few key quality issues that it will systematically address over time.

Illinois Valley Community College conducted a two-day self-assessment exercise that enabled it to identify the "IVCC Vital Few." These are the key strategic issues that will be the focal point for the community college's strategic planning and reaccreditation efforts with the Higher Learning Commission.[8]

EDUCATING ADMINISTRATIVE STAFF ORGANIZATIONS

For staff organizations, it is generally advisable to organize quality training workshops that involve the entire office group together, rather than sending individuals to different continuous improvement workshops. If an office cannot be shut down for everyone to be trained at once, then design the training so that half can attend the workshop one day and the other half on another day. The objective is to create a common understanding about continuous improvement among everyone in the group in a relatively short amount of time and to encourage and enable them to discuss the concepts among themselves and to apply the concepts and tools to their own work processes. When individuals attend continuous improvement workshops by themselves, they often have difficulty applying the concepts and tools back in the workplace, since no one else has attended. For example, the entire staff of the Registrar's Office at Alabama attended a one-day continuous improvement workshop together and was able to apply the tools to examples from their own office during the workshop.

Binghamton usually conducts a full-day or half-day workshop that brings everyone from a specific office together in a retreat setting—away from their work area. The session begins by brainstorming the strengths and areas for improvement. Participants then use nominal group technique to decide on the areas to work on. In some cases, people start working on process maps during the training session, and in other cases they identify the types of data that should be collected for further analysis to understand a process. An action plan is developed to guide the process for collecting data and for organizing follow-up sessions to review data. This approach helps people learn the continuous improvement concepts and tools on real, live issues. The action plan helps them to stay on task and to move forward.

The University of Texas–Austin provides a one-day Quality Tools and Techniques Workshop that covers brainstorming, flowcharting, Pareto diagrams, cause and effect diagrams, check sheets, Gantt charts, Nominal Group Techniques, and Force Field Analysis.[9]

Alabama designed a one-day workshop to teach continuous improvement tools and concepts to its administrative staff. The content included an introduction to basic improvement concepts, such as the Input-Process-Output model, the need to measure and understand variation in processes, and the need to have performance measures for work processes. Participants worked in teams to develop flowcharts for their own work processes and developed cause and effect diagrams around issues in their organization. The workshop introduced participants to forms of data collection, such as check sheets, data matrices, histograms, and Pareto charts, and to the concept of special cause and common cause variation.

Of course, it is the administrative unit's management that is responsible for encouraging the staff to utilize the continuous improvement tools after the training workshop. The staff in the Student Financial Aid office at Alabama flowcharted most of their work processes after training in order to smooth out process flows.

PREPARING A CADRE OF FACILITATORS

Widespread adoption of quality improvement across a research university requires the creation of numerous facilitators who can lead groups in a variety of processes. The University of Texas implemented a three-day workshop for facilitators. The workshop covered ground rules and operating procedures, active interventions and conflict management, communication skills and active listening, effective negotiations and consensus decision making, and group development concepts.

By creating facilitators throughout the campus, continuous improvement is not dependent on a staff organization. Over time, continuous improvement methods and philosophies become ingrained in the organization and become the concepts and tools that people normally use to administer the campus.

Binghamton offers a three-day training program for facilitators that covers the theory of teams; effective tools for team processes, such as brainstorming, nominal group technique, and process mapping; and con-flict management methods. Newly trained facilitators will shadow expe-rienced facilitators to observe, cofacilitate, and then facilitate with an experienced person observing them before facilitating on their own. Facilitators at Binghamton meet to discuss how they are progressing and how they feel about specific facilitation projects.

FACULTY AND EXECUTIVES

Many universities have developed short training modules that are used to acquaint a broader population on their campuses with quality concepts and methods.

Binghamton offers a summer workshop series that is built around the concept that everyone is a leader and that everyone can benefit from hav-ing good meetings and improved processes. Binghamton encourages any-one on their campus to participate in these workshops and employs the theme of "workplace renovations" to organize its series, with workshops on:

Laying the Foundation. Helps academic and administrative leaders learn how to get started with enhancing cooperation, communication, collabora-tion, problem solving, and conflict resolution.

Basic Tools. Guides people in gathering ideas from people and developing a consensus on which ideas to address first.

Power Tools. Focuses on diagnostic tools that help solve problems and improve processes.

The Roofing Party. Provides leaders with teambuilding skills and activities that build collaboration and teamwork within an organization.

The University of Texas provides leadership seminars such as:

The Manager as Coach. This course focuses on new behaviors and attitudes for managers to coach, empower, lead, and facilitate employees.

Managing for Performance Excellence. This course allows leaders to under-stand and use the Baldrige Award's seven-category assessment process. Participants will perform an organizational quality self-assessment.

Work Process Mapping. This course demonstrates the value of mapping a work process and helps people reevaluate existing processes.

Negotiation for Mutual Gain. This course teaches participants to focus on interests instead of positions and to develop partnership relationships.

Villanova has developed a series of Leadership Development Train-ing programs as part of its quality initiative. Nine modules are provided in the program, which engages supervisors from departments all across the campus. Topics include proactive listening, giving and receiving constructive feedback, collaboration, giving recognition, and coaching skills.

Alabama has developed a series of six three-hour modules available for faculty members and executives that are offered through open enrollment in the summer and during the fall and spring semesters that can also be scheduled as a faculty development program at any time during the year. Each module focuses on a specific set of concepts and tools that will benefit faculty and administrators in an academic department.

There is a significant advantage to having all the faculty in a department or college attend a workshop together, because it stimulates analysis, discussion, and ideas for application. After a couple of Nursing faculty members attended the workshop on Leading Participative Meetings, for example, the entire faculty of the College of Nursing at Alabama took the workshop together and had a lively discussion that has resulted in a redesign of the faculty meetings.

> *Leading Participative Meetings* examines the continuum of decision-making styles and helps leaders learn about a variety of agendas and techniques they can use to better organize and conduct meetings.
>
> *Consensus-Based Decision Making* addresses the use of nominal group technique to identify a consensus within a group and examines a rational model for decision making that emphasizes establishing agreement on objectives within a group before identifying, evaluating, and selecting alternatives.
>
> The *Planning Skills* workshop covers the development of action plans, the use of Gantt charts, and a rational process for identifying and addressing potential problems that may occur as a plan is implemented.
>
> The workshop on *Process Improvement* helps faculty and staff embrace a process improvement perspective toward student learning, grant applications, research projects, and advising, along with administrative functions such as ordering books, leading a search committee, and supervising a student's dissertation.
>
> The *Creative Thinking* workshop engages participants in creative thinking concepts and methods, including the use of mind maps, lateral thinking, and metaphorical thinking techniques.
>
> The workshop on *Conducting Self-Assessments* leads group members through an assessment of their academic or administrative department using the CQI short-form evaluation shown in Chapter 4.

QUALITY FORUMS AND SHOWCASES

People often learn about the uses and benefits of quality tools by seeing how other organizations have applied these tools in their part of the campus or on another campus. Several universities, such as Pennsylvania State University and the University of Wisconsin–Madison, conduct forums, or showcases, in which teams from across the campus present the results of their continuous quality improvement activities. The California State University System conducts an annual forum that brings together teams from Cal State campuses all across the state. A forum can range from ten to forty or more team displays that showcase the use of self-assessments, strategic planning, stakeholder surveys, process improvements, team-building projects, team-based applications of project management activities, and new breakthroughs in services.

The University of Michigan has conducted Quality Expos that combine training clinics with team exhibits. Clinic topics have included information on starting work teams, establishing self-managed teams, improving team meetings, and training on using quality indicators. Teams from the School of Dentistry, the Information Technology Division, Facilities, Human Resources, the Registrar's Office, housing, medical clinics, and many administrative offices have presented information on process improvements.

Quality Forums at The University of Alabama have included team displays from university libraries, the School of Social Work, the Mathematics Department, The Adult Learning Program, Admissions, Student Financial Aid, the Student Career Center, the Student Health Center, university recreation, university police, The Alabama Museum of Natural History, Transportation Services, Human Resources, and Maintenance.

Binghamton conducts an annual recognition luncheon, attended by the president and all the vice presidents to recognize each team that has been involved in an improvement activity that year. Each person who participated in a team activity is called out by name for recognition. Surveys of participants have found that this is a highly effective way to recognize both individual and team efforts for improvement. People appreciate the recognition from the senior administrators and the feeling that they are being given top-notch treatment in acknowledgement of their efforts.

Organizations recognized at Binghamton's Recognition Luncheon have included academic advisors, the campus Judicial Affairs office, the Career Development Center, the Chemistry Department faculty, the Environmental Health and Safety staff, International Student Scholar Services staff, the university Registrar's Office, the Office for Students with Disabilities, and many others.

NO INSTANT PUDDING!

W. Edwards Deming often remarked that, when it came to achieving excellence in an organization, there was no such thing as instant pudding, although that is what everyone wants. Continuous improvement requires an organized, systematic, and sustained effort in every setting.[10]

Phillip Crosby noted there is a cost to obtaining excellence. An organization must invest in training, flowcharting, data collection, analysis, and team meetings to improve processes and services to stakeholders. However, Crosby also observed that the cost of poor quality (students who leave because they are dissatisfied with teaching or administrative problems, grants that are not received due to a poor grant-writing process, alumni who withhold gifts because they are angry about their college experience, and potential students who do not apply or enroll due to the institution's poor reputation, for example) far outweighs the investment in continuous improvement.[11]

Continuous improvement initiatives in any setting—higher education, K–12 schools, health care, government, business, or industry—will fail when the leadership is unconsciously incompetent. The history of the continuous improvement movement shows that a systematic approach to improvement can be highly successful when led by consciously competent managers. Leaders who expect instant pudding will always be disappointed and will never accept responsibility when their improvement initiative does not provide instant results. A sustained investment in educating the campus about continuous improvement and encouraging people to apply the tools and to share their results will yield great dividends over time.

It can take seven to ten years to change a culture. People must be patient and gentle, because change can be a difficult thing. Organizations in higher education must remember to start with baby steps to experience small successes so that people do not feel overwhelmed and quit. For many administrators, it is a new experience to empower people and to entrust their staff.

At Binghamton the saying goes, "Leaders talk about the future. If you talk about the present, you are in the past—defending why you are doing the present."

NOTES

1. W. Edwards Deming, *Quality, Productivity, and Competitive Position* (Cambridge, MA: Massachusetts Institute of Technology, 1982).

2. Barbara Sherlock, "Teams Improve the Scheduling of Courses, the Handling of SRTE Forms and Audio Visual Support in Classrooms," Center for

Quality and Planning, Pennsylvania State University, in *Quality Endeavors*, January/February 2002.

3. Villanova University, Quality Activity Report, 2002.

4. Ronald Hunsinger, "Total Quality Improvement in the Basic Sciences," in *Quality Quest in the Academic Process*, Samford University and GOAL/QPC, 1992.

5. "Mapping the Progress of Process Mapping," Quality Improvement Newsletter for the California State University, January 2000.

6. Ibid.

7. Joseph Juran, *Managerial Breakthrough* (New York: McGraw-Hill, 1964).

8. Laurie Adolph and Harriet Howell Custer, "Field Notes from Two Trailbreakers," A Collection of Papers on Self-Study and Institutional Improvement, The Higher Learning Commission, Chicago, 2002.

9. The University of Texas Quality Center, fall, 1998.

10. Deming, *Quality, Productivity, and Competitive Position*.

11. Phillip J. Crosby, *Quality Is Free* (New York: Signet Books, 1979).

CHAPTER 4

Conducting Self-Assessments

The best assurance that an organization does quality work comes from examining its systems, processes, and its approaches to improving them continually.
—Stephen Spangehl, The Higher Learning Commission

As campuses ponder the concept of continuous improvement, people often ask: "Improvement of what?" The continuous improvement cycle places a strong emphasis on conducting self-assessments in order to identify the most important opportunities and areas that need to be addressed in order to meet the needs of the campus's stakeholders.

Self-assessments are a key ingredient in achieving and maintaining excellence in any educational setting. As a mechanism for stimulating a constructive critical analysis of an institution, self-assessments enable organizations to realistically acknowledge their strengths and weaknesses and set the stage for continuous improvement.

Educational institutions, as well as individuals, may be described as functioning within a model that contains four levels of critical self-awareness:

Consciously competent

Unconsciously competent

Consciously incompetent

Unconsciously incompetent

UNCONSCIOUS INCOMPETENCE

The unconsciously incompetent educational institution does a poor job in educating its students, but the faculty and administrators do not realize they are doing a poor job. They believe they are going through the same motions as everyone else; they believe they must be achieving about the same results as others, so they think they must be doing okay.

The unconsciously incompetent institution is perpetuated by a lack of performance feedback. Administrators and faculty do not take the opportunity to collect and study the comparative data available to them through national surveys, nor do they analyze test scores, admission rates of their undergraduates into graduate school, feedback from employers, or feedback from students on faculty evaluations. The institution does not go out of its way to collect additional data from students, parents, or employers.

In K–12 schools, the national trend for school accountability is focused on identifying the unconscious incompetent schools and helping the schools become aware of their incompetence. In higher education, comparative data on student results on standardized tests has only recently become available. For example, universities have only been able to compare the performance of their graduates on the Graduate Record Exam with the national scores for the students who took the examination beginning in 2000. Because there are no standardized national examinations for graduates of community colleges, there is no comparative data to evaluate outcomes. Community colleges can, however, obtain feedback from the four-year schools to which their students transfer regarding their performance and can utilize the ACT Alumni Outcome Survey to obtain comparative data.

CONSCIOUS INCOMPETENCE

It is a significant step for an institution to become conscious of its incompetence. Until this happens, there will be no systematic effort to improve within the unconscious incompetent institution because there is no perceived need for improvement.

When an institution becomes conscious of its incompetence, it begins to recognize deficiencies. At the conscious incompetence level, an institution can recognize the gaps in its practices, performance, and results and can begin to make plans for improvement.

How does an institution move from unconscious incompetence to conscious incompetence? This can happen through an external review, such as reaccreditation. However, it is unfortunate for the realization to occur in this manner because the institution is then under external pressure to improve and may receive bad publicity that hurts the students and faculty.

It is far better to make the transition through other means, such as the use of an institutional report card (see Chapter 9), the creation and use of operational performance measures in each academic unit (see Chapter 9), and through self-assessments that evaluate the institution against established criteria.

The goal of the consciously incompetent institution should be to move itself to the level of conscious competence. This will require "constancy of purpose" among the senior leadership.

UNCONSCIOUS COMPETENCE

Some institutions may be described as unconsciously competent. They are good, but if asked what causes them to be good, they would be hard pressed to explain their performance. Unconscious competence is often due to the dedicated expertise of a few individuals whose personal excellence keeps things moving in an effective manner. If the upper administration is not critically aware of the factors that are making an organization successful, they may unwittingly initiate changes that cause the organization to begin to fail. Success may be due to an individual faculty member who devotes additional hours to advising and mentoring students. It could be a registrar who has thirty years of experience and keeps the office performing well despite institutional problems.

The problem with unconscious competence is that it often hinges on personalities or conditions that are not recognized and not replicated throughout the institution. Eventually, the person who holds it all together will leave the institution and, at that point, the organization may unknowingly slip into incompetent performance.

When an institution performs competently but is not critically self-aware as to why it performs so well, it is wise to ask why. How will the institution ensure that it can continue to do well? How can it expand its strengths throughout the organization?

CONSCIOUS COMPETENCE

Conscious competence describes the institution that is performing well, shows good results, and understands its internal work process and decision-making processes. The leadership at the consciously competent organization is constantly assessing the institution to ensure that it improves further and anticipates potential problems in performance.

Consciously competent organizations often maintain an institutional report card that gives feedback from a variety of stakeholders. The institution has identified and keeps performance indicators for each academic and administrative group to understand long-term performance trends. This organization will often assess itself against national criteria for excellence in higher education.

STARTING WITH A MODEL

The self-assessment process can begin with an exercise as simple as drawing a model that describes the management system of the institution. The management system is the manner in which an organization collects data and makes decisions regarding the life of the institution. A model of the management system allows members of the institution to visually assess the manner in which information is collected, evaluated, and used to guide decisions made for the institution.

Figure 4.1 is a model of the management system for a campus. This model illustrates the manner in which the president and executive staff manage two loops of information: an external loop and an internal loop. The executives gather and assess information from external sources, use feedback from internal sources, and initiate actions that propel the institution in one direction or another. The model can be explained in the following manner.

External input begins with the institution's Board of Trustees. Depending on the institution's structure, this board could include representatives from a state's congressional districts, the state superintendent of education, and the governor of the state. If the university or college is affiliated with a religious institution, the board could include church officials, and members could all be appointed by the religious institution.

The president and executive staff will review a variety of comparative operational data, including comparisons of tuition with competing institutions, comparison of enrollment data with competing institutions, comparison of research funding with competing universities, national peer rankings, comparative data (such as the information produced through the University of Delaware's studies), and comparative data produced through the National Association of College and University Business Officers (NACUBO), or other professional associations.

In addition, the president and executive staff study various external quality reviews of the institution, including peer reviews of academic programs, accreditation of administrative programs, such as the student health center, and review of academic program viability by state agencies if it is a public community college, college, or university.

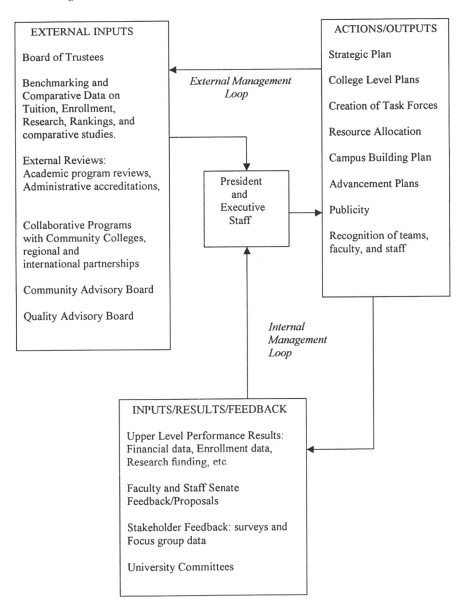

Figure 4.1 Executive Level Management System

The president and executive staff may communicate directly with the presidents of other campuses in the state or region to develop and sustain collaborative ventures.

Internal inputs and performance feedback come to the president and executive staff through multiple channels. The president needs a set of upper level key performance indicators that enables trend analysis in strategic areas, such as research, diversity, and advancement.

A faculty or staff senate will provide a comprehensive voice for the interests of the faculty and/or staff, giving the president direct recommendations and providing guidance through multiple committees. In most institutions, faculty and staff also participate on standing committees that provide internal input into decision making.

Any campus, whether a community college, small liberal arts college, regional university, or research university, should systematically conduct surveys and other feedback processes that give stakeholder feedback to the president and executive staff. A comprehensive report card that integrates feedback from students, parents, faculty, staff, and alumni can give the president and executive staff a broad view of stakeholder input and ideas for new improvement initiatives.

The president and executive staff can make increasing use of national surveys that provide comparative data regarding student performance outcomes, such as the National Survey of Student Engagement and the ACT's Alumni Outcomes Survey.

The president and executive staff integrate this external and internal feedback in their meetings and should provide leadership through the issuance of a strategic plan that establishes strategic objectives that are incorporated in each college and administrative unit's strategic plan. The president and executive staff then charter task forces to address quality issues that cross campus boundaries. The president and executive staff decide on resource allocations to support the mission and the strategic plan, and oversee the campus building plans that likewise support the strategic directions of the university. Advancement and publicity initiatives come from the president and executive staff through analysis of stakeholder surveys and needs assessments, as well as public recognition for faculty and staff for performance excellence.

Figure 4.2 shows the management system for a typical college, led by a dean, within a major university. External input for the college flows down from the university's strategic plan. Each college reviews comparative data from its own benchmarking studies, as well as comparative data, such as information from the University of Delaware study, the National Survey of Student Engagement, and the ACT's Alumni Outcome Survey. Each college will usually have some type of Board of Visitors who represent the voice of the many stakeholder groups, including alumni and agencies or companies that hire graduates and fund research. Additionally, major academic programs undergo a periodic external quality audit conducted by a peer review process, in most cases under the auspices of an independent national accrediting organization.

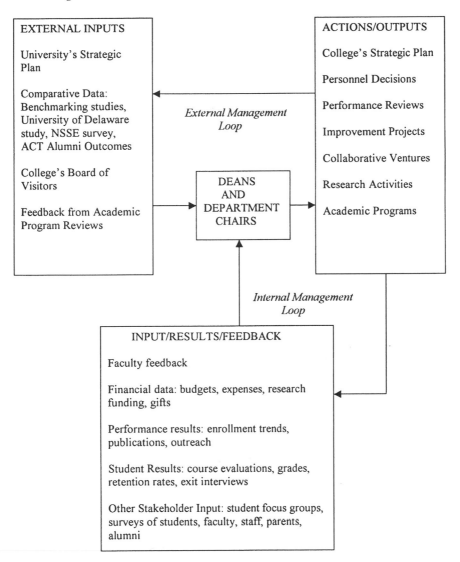

Figure 4.2   College Level Management System

Deans and department chairs review a variety of internal feedback and results data as part of the management system. Faculty members provide structured performance feedback for department chairs and deans. Deans and chairs receive monthly financial performance data related to budgets, expenses, research funding, and gifts. Deans evaluate performance results, such as enrollment trends, faculty publications, research grants, and participation in service activities. Student results are reviewed through course evaluations, comparative grades from classes, performance on standardized exams, alumni response to comparative outcome surveys, and exit interviews with graduates. Deans obtain additional stakeholder input from student focus groups, surveys of students, faculty, staff, parents, and alumni.

At the college level, the deans incorporate the external and internal inputs to formulate strategic plans and actions. Strategic plans are developed with faculty input and are reviewed by the provost. Staffing and promotional decisions are driven by performance results and student results. Deans and/or department chairs conduct formal evaluations with faculty on an annual basis, based on performance results. Deans initiate improvement projects based on performance results and establish collaborative ventures with other colleges.

Figure 4.3 illustrates the management system for administrative organizations, such as student services, academic support organizations, administrative functions, and outreach programs.

Vice presidents and directors in administrative organizations review a variety of external comparative data obtained through professional organizations, consultants, benchmarking, and NACUBO. Some of the university's administrative functions are engaged in external quality assessments, such as the U.S. Department of Education's Quality Assurance Program for student financial aid.

Internal feedback and results come from performance indicators that are specific to each group, from stakeholder surveys, and from an internal self-assessment process based on the Malcolm Baldrige National Quality Award criteria.

Vice presidents and directors use the external and internal process feedback to develop strategic plans, to launch improvement projects, to initiate benchmarking visits, to provide performance reviews for staff, to fuel the recognition system, and to identify needs and opportunities for staff training and development.

Creating a model of the institution's management system helps people visually connect the flow of information and types of decision making that lead to conscious competence. A model helps leaders determine the types of stakeholder data that should be obtained to have comprehensive feedback. The model also helps establish the types of operational indicators that should be in place for each academic unit and each administrative support function.

COMPRESSING THESE MODELS

All these models are compressed when considering the management system of a four-year college or a community college. In smaller institu-

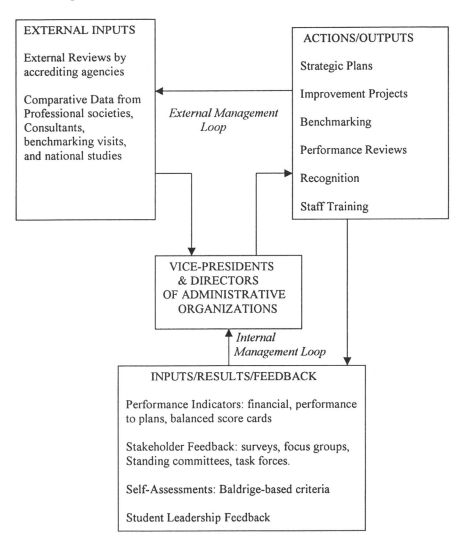

Figure 4.3 Administrative Management System

tions, the management activities are carried out by fewer levels of managers, who often wear multiple hats. The role of dean disappears in many four-year colleges where the vice president for academic affairs has a multitude of academic programs reporting directly to him or her with no role played by deans. Administrative functions may be combined so that a single individual has oversight for a wide range of student activities or administrative duties.

Regardless of the size of the institution, it requires a management system. In many organizations, managers simply manage without any critical awareness or reflection on what they are doing or how it might be done more effectively.

The purpose of a model is to help managers in higher education settings start to define how their existing management system functions and to consider ways in which it could be improved.

EVALUATING AGAINST A STANDARD

It is difficult to determine an organization's performance and to measure improvement without the use of some type of yardstick or standard against which to measure. If an organization compares itself to the personal standards of a president or the members of a Board of Trustees, then the standard will change every few years according to the perspective of the individuals involved. This will cause the organization to bounce from one initiative to another without any consistent long-term progress.

For long-term, sustained improvement, an institution needs to compare itself to a nationally recognized standard that has been developed through some type of consensus process. Comparing an institution's management system to a consensus standard may be an approach that emerges over time as an institution enters into a mature phase in its continuous improvement efforts, or it may be an approach initiated early in order to provide focus on improving core institutional processes.

There are two systematic consensus standards to evaluate the quality of higher educational institutions currently in use. First, the Malcolm Baldrige National Quality Award for Education has been in use for several years. The Baldrige Award criteria for education is being used by many state quality-award programs to provide a structure for self-assessment in K–12 and higher education. The American Society for Quality, along with several consulting firms, offers workshops to introduce college leaders to the Baldrige criteria. Many states have trained assessors who can coach colleges and universities in using the Baldrige criteria for self-evaluation.

The North Central Association of Colleges and Schools recently initiated the Academic Quality Improvement Project (AQIP) that developed a set of assessment criteria similar to the Baldrige Award criteria, but more tailored for higher education. Under the AQIP model, schools conduct a self-assessment and develop an improvement plan based on the needs they have identified. The schools work on their improvement plan and then reassess themselves to develop new improvement goals. When the association sees evidence that this cycle of continuous improvement is in place, it will grant reaccreditation to the institution.

In many cases it is a big step to jump in and start evaluating an institution, or even one academic department or administrative unit, against the Baldrige criteria or the AQIP criteria. Performing a self-assessment against all of the criteria in the Baldrige can take weeks. While full use of a Baldrige-based self-assessment may be the goal of an institution, it is often effective to introduce self-assessment through the use of a short form. Figure 4.4 is a self-assessment short form that reflects the seven criteria of the Malcolm Baldrige National Quality Award in a few basic questions. Academic and administrative leaders have used this form to stimulate discussion and to begin to encourage people to ask questions that lead to critical self-examination. In most cases, a team will assess their organization using the short form and come to the conclusion that they are in the early stages of understanding quality. It is easy to overwhelm people in the early stages of an improvement initiative. Requiring a team to conduct a self-assessment with all the Baldrige criteria at the beginning of the quality initiative may overload the organization. It is often better to get administrators, faculty, and staff used to self-assessment through the use of a short form and to start making improvements. Over time, as people have some success and the concepts begin to sink in, it becomes much easier to organize and lead a more comprehensive self-assessment process.

COMPARING AN INSTITUTION AGAINST THE BALDRIGE CRITERIA

The Malcolm Baldrige National Quality Award criteria and a variety of state-level quality awards that are widely used across the country are designed to stimulate critical thinking about the manner in which the institution manages itself.

To conduct a self-assessment using the Baldrige criteria (or a state-level version of the Baldrige) the institution should create a self-assessment team. If the institution already has a Quality Council in place, it is very appropriate for the Quality Council to conduct the self-assessment. The idea is to engage a broad spectrum of people in conducting the self-assessment. The self-assessment process is very educational and will motivate people to support improvements. The usefulness of the self-assessment is greatly diminished if it is conducted by a small group of administrators or by an individual.

The purpose of the self-assessment is to propel an organization along the path of continuous improvement, not to win an award. The desire to

Where is your organization on the CI journey? Circle the point on each scale that best describes your organization. Add up your scores in all 7 areas.

1. *Status of your strategic plan.*

No strategic Plan exists	Strategic plan is in place	Have had a plan for several years	Have a mature strategic planning process	
0	2	4	5	_____ score

2. Status of your mission statement

No mission Statement Exists	We're getting ready to prepare one	Have a M.S. that focuses on actions	M. S. focuses on accomplishments & is visible.	
0	2	4	5	_____ score

3. Status of Stakeholder Satisfaction Data

Have no Stakeholder Data	Starting to collect data	Collect data but don't use it.	Collect & use some data	Regularly use data from stakeholders	
0	5	10	20	25	_____ score

(Stakeholders might be students, organizations that hire our graduates, graduate programs that recruit our students, organizations that fund research, parents of students, faculty, and staff)

4. Status of key performance measures.

Have not identified a set of key measures	Starting to establish key measures	Collecting data on key measures	Have data on key measures	Key measures data posted for all to see/use.	
0	5	10	15	20	_____ score

5. Status on process improvement

Major processes have not been identified	Major processes identified	Some processes have flow charts	All major processes flow charted	Measures show improvements in major processes	
0	5	10	15	20	_____ score

6. Benchmarking status

Do not know who is the best in our field	Have identified areas where we need to conduct benchmarking	Have started a systematic benchmarking program	Other organizations benchmark us because we are one of the best in our field.	
0	3	6	10	_____ score

Figure 4.4   Continuous Improvement Self-Assessment Instrument

7. Status of leadership

Not interested in CI issues	Beginning to show interest in CI	Have attended CI workshop	Have attended most leadership seminars that support CI	
				_____score
0	3	6	10	

Total Score _____

Add up the scores for your organization in all 7 areas for a total score.

0-20:   The organization is new to the concepts of CI.

21-40: The organization has just started on the CI journey.

41-60: The organization is making progress with CI.

61-80: The organization is demonstrating leadership in applying CI principles.

81-100: The organization has a very mature understanding and use of CI concepts.

Figure 4.4   (Continued)

receive recognition for continuous improvement may motivate leaders to use self-assessments as part of their quality improvement strategy, but the benefits come from being on the journey, not in trying to reach a destination. Corporations that have won the Baldrige Award all echo this view. The benefits derived from conducting self-assessments and developing plans for improvement far outweigh the benefits of public recognition.

The Baldrige criteria encourage the institution to examine itself critically in seven categories. The titles of these categories have changed somewhat since the criteria were introduced in the 1980s, but they remain basically the same. The self-assessment team will be asked to examine how the organization's leadership functions, how the strategic planning process is managed, how the institution focuses on the needs of students and other stakeholders, how the institution uses information, how it deals with faculty and staff, the manner in which the educational process and support processes are managed, and how the organization addresses performance results.[1]

Leadership

In the leadership area, the Baldrige criteria encourages the assessment team to consider how the institution's senior leaders guide the overall management system. This includes how they shape organizational values and how they establish performance expectations. The assessment team must consider how the leadership focuses on students and other stakeholders, how they measure and encourage student learning, and how they empower faculty and staff.

In the assessment of leadership, the team is asked to describe how senior leaders guide the organization and review organizational performance. They begin by examining how the leadership establishes a clear mission, articulates core values, and communicates high expectations for performance. The team must examine how senior leaders create and sustain an educational environment that promotes ethical values and equity for all students in a safe setting. The team will consider how the senior leaders encourage innovation and pursue current and future opportunities for improvement.

It is important for the self-assessment process to consider the manner in which senior leaders review the overall performance of the institution. The team will look at how the leaders assess the health of the organization, how they compare the organization's performance with other comparable organizations, and how they determine whether progress is being made on improvement activities.

In the self-assessment process, the team will evaluate the extent to which the senior leadership has conducted reviews of the organization's performance, established priorities for improvement, and collaborated with feeder and/or receiving schools, suppliers and key stakeholders to ensure that the organization's mission is successfully achieved. The self-assessment team will be asked to determine how well the senior leaders are using feedback from faculty and staff to improve their leadership effectiveness and the effectiveness of management throughout the organization.

The Leadership section of the Baldrige criteria also encourages examination of the manner in which the institution addresses its responsibilities to the public and practices good citizenship. The team will consider how the institution addresses potential safety and regulatory risks and how it anticipates public concerns regarding its operation. The process also stimulates inquiry regarding the way in which the leadership ensures ethical practices in all student and stakeholder interactions.

Strategic Planning

The self-assessment team will examine the organization's process for developing strategic plans, action plans, and plans that impact faculty and staff resources. In this part of the self-assessment, the team will be required to define the institution's strategic planning process and to show how the institution considers key factors, such as student needs and expectations, changing external factors, new technology, budgetary constraints, the needs and capabilities of faculty and staff, and other resource needs.

The self-assessment team will examine the extent to which the institution has established key objectives and has a timetable for accomplishing them. The institution should have action plans for achieving its key objectives and should be able to articulate the faculty and resource needs to implement the action plans. The institution should have key performance measures, or milestones, to track the progress relative to the action plans, and should be able to show evidence of effectively communicating the plan to faculty and staff.

Student and Stakeholder Performance

This section of the Baldrige education criteria enables the self-assessment team to scrutinize the manner in which the institution determines its performance requirements and expectations based on input from students and stakeholders and the extent to which the organization effectively builds relationships with students and stakeholders and listens to them to determine their level of satisfaction.

The team will be asked to consider how the institution maintains an awareness of student and stakeholder needs and satisfaction. They will look at how needs and expectations are determined and analyzed and how this information is shared with the appropriate groups on campus. The team will examine how the institution monitors student use of course offerings, facilities, and services. Additionally, the team will study the manner in which the organization considers demographic data and trends; changing requirements for graduates; changing national, state, or regional requirements; and how the institution factors these potential changes into its planning and operations.

The self-assessment team will consider the manner in which the institution obtains feedback from students and involves them in the campus to encourage retention and to enhance their performance. The team will determine what key indicators or measures are used to determine student satisfaction and what process the institution uses for resolving complaints. The team will look for evidence that the institution is effectively obtaining student satisfaction data and look for evidence of systematic use of these data to improve student services.

Information and Analysis

In this portion of the assessment criteria, the team examines the institution's performance measurement system and how the school analyzes its performance data and information. The team will describe how the organization maintains effective performance measurement systems for understanding and improving performance at all levels and throughout the organization. The manner in which measures and indicators are selected and tracked will be considered by the team, as well as the extent to which the school uses comparative data and information. These data may come from other academic institutions or from outside academe, as in the operation of auxiliary services, financial services, security, and other support functions.

The self-assessment team will review the manner in which data and information are assessed throughout the organization. This includes how the senior leadership uses data to assess overall performance, how student performance data are assessed and used, daily use of operational data, and the manner in which data are provided to faculty and staff for program evaluation and improvement.

Faculty and Staff

The category related to faculty and staff enables the team to examine how the institution provides a climate conducive to excellence, personal and organizational growth, and full participation in a manner consistent with the organization's mission and objectives.

The self-assessment team will consider how the institution promotes teamwork and individual excellence through its design, organization, and management of jobs for faculty and staff. The team will reflect on how the administrators encourage and motivate faculty and staff and obtain faculty and staff feedback. Compensation, recognition, rewards, and incentives will all be considered by the team, along with hiring practices, fair workforce practices, and diversity.

The manner in which the school supports faculty and staff education, training, and development will also be considered by the self-assessment team. The team will review how the organization addresses certification, licensure, development, and learning needs for faculty and staff. They will want to determine how the school delivers workshops and training, along with other professional and technical development.

In this section, the self-assessment team examines how the organization addresses and improves workplace health and safety, including ergonomic needs. The team looks at how faculty and staff are involved in determining health, safety, and environmental concerns. The team also looks at the formal and informal evaluation methods used by the school to determine faculty and staff well-being, satisfaction, and motivation.

Educational and Support Process Management

Here, the self-assessment team examines the processes used for designing and delivering educational programs. The team will determine how programs are designed and how the school ensures that these programs meet high standards while fully addressing the students' individual needs. The manner in which the school incorporates changing requirements and new technology in program design will be considered by the team. Team members will also study how faculty and staff are prepared to implement educational programs.

The team will ask questions to determine how the institution ensures that its educational programs meet their design and delivery requirements. How are courses monitored, and how do faculty and students receive feedback in order to be successful? The team will look for examples related to how the institution makes use of research on learning, assessment, and improved instructional methods and learning technology.

Educational support processes are also examined in this section. The team will define the institution's key educational support processes and see if students, faculty, staff, and other stakeholders have had appropriate input in determining the performance requirements for these processes. The team will then go on to determine if the processes meet the requirements and will look at how the organization systematically improves these processes.

This section of the Baldrige criteria also calls upon the team to describe how the organization partners with other schools and places of work, as appropriate. This includes partnering with the schools that provide applicants and those that accept graduates. These partnerships also include working with the companies that hire graduates.

Organizational Performance and Results

In this category, the team examines the results of the institution's educational programs. The team reviews current levels and trends in student performance, student and stakeholder satisfaction trends, budgetary and financial results, faculty and staff satisfaction, and safety results. The team looks at evidence that indicates that the school is effective in enhancing

the learning of students and in accomplishing other parts of its core mission, such as research and service to the community.

EVALUATING AN INSTITUTION WITH AQIP

The North Central Association of Colleges and Schools has moved the
methodology for conducting self-assessments beyond the Baldrige criteria
by establishing a set of quality criteria customized for higher education.
Through the Academic Quality Improvement Project (AQIP) criteria,
schools can conduct a holistic self-assessment that examines issues related
to the institution's management system and performance. The North
Central Association's AQIP team has identified nine broad criteria. The
institution that uses the AQIP criteria should look at itself as a whole in
terms of how it meets these nine criteria. As in the Baldrige Award self-
assessment, schools using the AQIP model will consider a variety of
questions that are designed to help stimulate constructive critical self-
assessment. These questions will help schools identify their strengths and
the areas where they need to work on improvement. As in the Baldrige
self-assessment process, a school would assemble a self-evaluation team
to consider the nine criteria.[2]

The nine AQIP criteria are:

1. *Helping Students Learn.* This criterion helps the school examine inter-
    nal processes for developing and reviewing academic programs, instruc-
    tional delivery, and the whole process of assessing student performance.
    The self-evaluation team will consider the admissions and records
    processes, and will assess how student activities, advising, counseling,
    and residential life support the goals of student learning.

2. *Accomplishing Other Distinctive Objectives.* This criterion encourages
    reflection on the manner in which the institution manages financial
    resources, conducts research, provides outreach to the community, and
    ensures integrity in auxiliary activities, such as athletics.

3. *Understanding Students' and Other Stakeholders' Needs.* In this criterion,
    the self-assessment team considers how the institution identifies and
    assesses the needs of students and other stakeholders, how performance
    targets are established for students, and how the institution deals with
    the public and other stakeholder groups, such as parents, alumni, em-
    ployers, and state and federal governments.

4. *Valuing People* is the fourth criterion for self-assessment. This criterion
    focuses the team on how the institution develops the capabilities of the
    faculty, staff, and administration; how the institution designs and evalu-
    ates its systems for recruiting training, developing, recognizing, and

listening to faculty and staff; and how the valuing of faculty and staff contributes to the goal of helping students learn.

5. The fifth criterion *Leading and Communicating*, examines the leadership system from the trustees down through day-to-day supervision. Questions in this section encourage discussion regarding how strategic directions are set; how decisions are made; and how the institution communicates its values, directions, and expectations.

6. *Supporting Institutional Operations* enables the self-assessment team to examine the institution's support processes. This includes processes that are close to the students, such as financial aid, libraries, classroom support, work-study, and registration as well as processes that the students may rarely see, such as procurement, capital campaigns, and administrative services. This criterion stimulates thinking about how these support processes are managed, evaluated, and improved.

7. The *Measuring Effectiveness* criterion requires the self-assessment team to look at the system used by the institution for collecting and using data for effective decision making. The team will determine if the institution has a systematic approach to collecting and using data and study how data are used to identify opportunities for continuous improvement.

8. The AQIP criterion includes a section on *Planning Continuous Improvement*, which pushes the self-assessment team to study how the institution compares its actual performance to its mission and stated goals. The team will ask how the institution evaluates itself and how it goes about the process of continuously identifying and initiating activities that will lead to further improvement.

9. In this final criterion, the self-assessment team examines the topic of *Building Collaborative Relationships*. Here, the self-assessment team examines how the institution encourages internal collaboration among faculty and academic departments, how it encourages collaboration with schools that provide students, how it collaborates with organizations that hire its graduates, and how it collaborates with community organizations and national educational bodies.

Together, these nine criteria create a comprehensive framework for examining the management system of a higher educational institution. The types of questions in each criterion compel the self-assessment team to ask difficult questions that will create beneficial critical analysis.

SOUTHERN ASSOCIATION'S QUALITY ENHANCEMENT PLANS

Like the North Central Association, the Southern Association of Colleges and Schools (SACS) has examined quality improvement methods and is seeking to embed them in the reaccreditation process.

Whereas the North Central Association is providing two paths to re-accreditation—the traditional path oriented toward quality assurance and a new path that emphasizes quality improvement—SACS is incorporating a quality improvement requirement into its new reaccreditation, or reaffirmation, process.[3]

Eight schools participated in a pilot project in 2001 to include a Quality Enhancement Plan in their self-assessment process. East Tennessee State University, for example, identified three improvement projects related to increasing student engagement for new freshmen, transfer students, and off-campus students.

The new SACS approach still requires each institution to prepare an institutional profile, but institutions are encouraged to make this a virtual document. SACS staff will still conduct a site visit and a compliance audit but will use Web documents posted by institutions to obtain much of their information.

MIDDLE STATES COMMISSION ON HIGHER EDUCATION

Middle States has likewise migrated to an assessment approach that emphasizes comprehensive outcomes assessment plans for its institutions.[4] The criteria for these plans include:

linkage of outcomes to the institution's mission, goals, and objectives;

support and collaboration of faculty and administration;

use of assessment and evaluation approaches that lead to improvement;

realistic goals and a timetable for accomplishing goals, along with appropriate investment; and

an evaluation of the assessment program.

Components of this assessment process establish a firm structure for continuous improvement in member institutions and include the hallmark of continuous improvement thinking in the requirement to evaluate the assessment process. This reflective thinking leads to a deeper understanding of an institution's management system.

EXCELLENCE IN HIGHER EDUCATION

Rutgers University has developed a version of the Baldrige criteria that is tailored to the higher education setting.[5] The Excellence in Higher

Education self-assessment process enables colleges and universities to examine their practices in:

Leadership

Planning

Service orientation

Information and analysis

Faculty, staff, and workplace climate

Process management

Excellence levels and trends

The Excellence in Higher Education process provides the campus with a structure for self-assessment, prioritization and planning of improvements, implementation of improvements, and the completion, celebration, and evaluation of the effectiveness of improvement efforts.

PACESETTER AWARD PROCESS

The PACESETTER award process was established by members of the Continuous Quality Improvement Network (CQIN) for Community and Technical Colleges in the late 1990s. The PACESETTER award criteria is based on the Baldrige criteria but has been tailored more specifically to community college and technical college needs.[6]

Schools using the PACESETTER award can start by conducting a shorter self-assessment using CQIN's Trailblazer Guide, which permits schools to become familiar with the PACESETTER criteria but does not require a lengthy application procedure. Schools can conduct a self-assessment using the Trailblazer Guide in two to four weeks and will receive feedback from CQIN's examiners.

Schools that desire a more in-depth self-assessment can complete the full PACESETTER self-assessment and can have examiners visit their campus and provide full feedback. The PACESETTER process seeks examiners who have already been trained to conduct evaluations using state-level Baldrige programs.

FOCUSED ASSESSMENTS

Although the self-assessment process is extremely valuable for assessing an institution's management system, campuses can also benefit from

Table 4.1
EHS List of Services

Rate each service on a 1 (ineffective/poor) to 5 (highly effective) scale:

Service	Rating
1. Laboratory Safety	_____
2. Hazardous Waste Management	_____
3. Universal Waste Management	_____
4. Emergency Response	_____
5. Training	_____
6. Fire Safety	_____
7. OSHA/PESH Program Management	_____
8. Bio-Safety	_____
9. Construction Industry Standard	_____
10. Permit Management	_____
11. Inspection/Audits	_____
12. Industrial Hygiene	_____
13. Document Review	_____
14. Outreach/Education	_____
15. EPA Preparation	_____
16. Internal Services	_____

---

tightly focused assessment in specific areas. Focused assessments are particularly useful in areas that require compliance to external requirements, such as adherence to the "Common Rule" for research projects, conformance to Equal Opportunity laws, and compliance to health, safety, and environmental regulations. Focused assessments are generally structured around the use of an assessment check sheet that provides structure in reviewing organizational performance. Table 4.1 is an example of a self-assessment guide for environmental, health, and safety compliance at Binghamton.

LINKING SELF-ASSESSMENTS TO STRATEGIC PLANNING

A thorough self-assessment, using the Baldrige or the AQIP criteria, can provide valuable input for an institution's strategic planning process.

Self-assessment helps the institution acknowledge its strengths and identify opportunities for improvement. Administrators, faculty, and staff can work together to develop plans to improve the management system to improve the results that the institution seeks to achieve.

In some settings, the challenge may be to acknowledge that the institution actually does many things very well. In the day-to-day work experience, people can become worn out and disenchanted with their work situation. The grass may often look greener at another institution. In some cases, faculty and staff are doing an excellent job, but have difficulty in acknowledging their own good performance. Self-assessments help identify the good features that should be maintained and celebrated.

In other cases, there are problems that are denied within the organization. It may not be considered safe, by the faculty and staff, to raise certain issues. A structured self-assessment process encourages an open review of the entire management system. In some cases, self-assessment enables people to articulate a problem in a manner that could never before be described.

In all cases, a thorough self-assessment, using a structured set of criteria, provides an important perspective for developing strategic and tactical plans for any college, community college, or university.

SUMMARY

While institutions can certainly benefit from the formation of a wide number of teams that address immediate and obvious problems for various stakeholder groups on a campus, a long-term commitment to continuous improvement soon moves the campus into the area of conducting self-assessments. Self-assessments are much more effective when they are based on a consensus standard that describes an effective approach to managing campus processes. Through self-assessment, institutions identify areas that require the development of new strategies, often setting the stage for the strategic planning process.

NOTES

1. National Institute of Standards and Technology, *Education Criteria for Performance Excellence*, Gaithersburg, MD, 2002.

2. Higher Learning Commission, *AQIP Quality Criteria*, Chicago, IL, 2001.

3. Southern Association of Colleges and Schools, *Principles of Accreditation: Foundations for Quality Enhancement*, Atlanta, GA, 2003.

4. Middle States Commission on Higher Education, www.msache.org/pubord.html.

5. Jennifer K. Lehr and Brent D. Ruben, "Excellence in Higher Education: A Baldrige-Based Self-Assessment Guide for Higher Education," *Assessment Update* 11, no. 1 (January/February 1999).

6. Laurie Adolph and Harriet Howell Custer, "Field Notes from Two Trailbreakers: Lessons Learned Using the CQIN Trailblazer for Self-Assessment," in *A Collection of Papers on Self-Study and Institutional Improvement*, The Higher Learning Commission of the North Central Association of Colleges and Schools, 2002.

CHAPTER

Strategic Planning:
Engaging Faculty and Staff

It is time for the university to start doing some things differently—
not just doing the same things better.

—David Ward

Many academic and administrative groups in higher education identify their needs for continuous improvement through the development of a strategic plan. As faculty and administrators develop their strategies, they often identify processes that will need to be improved in order to achieve their goals. Strategic planning encourages faculty and staff to listen to the voices of their stakeholders and to assess the strengths and weaknesses of their organization. All these activities help set the stage for systematic continuous improvement.

The perspective that continuous improvement brings to strategic planning is the need for a clearly defined process for strategic planning to which the institution adheres with some constancy of purpose while improving the process over time. It is not enough to conduct some type of strategic planning—usually when there is a change in upper administration. Rather, a strategic planning process needs to be clearly defined and woven into the institution's management system.

The University of Wisconsin–Stout provides a showcase model for a clearly defined and highly effective strategic planning model. The Stout model describes the makeup of the strategic planning team, the process they use, the frequency of the strategic planning activity, and the manner in which their faculty senate and staff senate are engaged in the process. This clear definition of process ensures that comprehensive planning, which includes faculty and staff, occurs on a regular basis.[1] Moreover, UW–Stout does a highly effective job of integrating its strategic planning process with the budgeting process. With an espoused set of values about "open and democratic" budgeting, the Stout campus keeps open communication with faculty in a year-round budgeting process that includes open forums for faculty input and posting of data about budget decisions. UW–Stout maintains a strong program for linking institutional plans with budgeted resources.[2]

The strategic planning process in the academic community differs significantly from strategic planning in the corporate setting. There are differences in terms of who needs to be involved in the planning process and differences in the relative emphasis on financial issues. There are similarities in terms of the need to develop a vision and to focus on a relatively small number of critical steps that will move the organization toward achieving the vision. Educational institutions and corporations can both have difficulties due to their mission statements.

Effective strategic planning in the educational setting combines aspects of planning from the corporate setting with the elements of the highly participative community planning process known as "future search." The future search process was created to enable a large number of people in a community or organization to have a voice in the strategic direction of their group.[3] The community-building feature of the future search conference is a vital component of strategic planning in education, where it is essential for a community of educators and stakeholders to develop a consensus regarding their collective future.

People who participate in strategic planning may have a negative view about the process due to past experiences. Strategic planning is often a long, drawn-out process that results in a document that commits the organization to a myriad of actions that no one finds compelling. The plan often ends up on a shelf gathering dust. To be effective, the strategic planning process needs to be fast paced, energetic, and result in a plan that people are excited about implementing.

WHO NEEDS TO BE INVOLVED IN STRATEGIC PLANNING?

Where the strategic planning process in the corporate setting may be exclusive, bringing together a small number of experts who can study market conditions, marketing data, and financial data, the educational setting moves toward the opposite extreme. Academic units, colleges, and universities need a broadly inclusive process in order for the plan to gain validity and commitment. A corporation may not share its strategic plan with its employees or even the stockholders. In education, the success of the plan usually depends on the understanding and commitment of the faculty, staff, students, and alumni. If a major stakeholder group feels cut out of the planning process, they may resist the implementation of the plan in a variety of unpredictable ways.

In an academic department, all of the faculty members need to be involved in developing a strategic plan. This plan will impact the teaching, research, and outreach activities of each faculty member, so they all need to have a voice in the planning process. Planning sessions need to be scheduled at a time when all faculty can attend. Many academic units have some type of factions within the faculty. It could be based on area of academic interest, philosophical differences, differences in research or teaching styles, or outside activity. It is important that all the faculty be included.

At some point, an organization becomes so large that all the faculty members cannot be present in the same room at the same time. When it becomes evident that everyone cannot be personally included, it is time to develop a strategic planning team in which everyone will be represented. If a college is made up of five academic departments, then each department needs representation, both from the chair and from faculty within the department. Administrative staff in the college also need a voice in the planning process, along with representatives from the students and the alumni. These diverse perspectives enrich the planning process and help ensure an outcome that will be well received by all stakeholder groups.

Academic support organizations also need strategic plans. Residential life, student health, financial aid, and the registrar's office must all deal with changing technology, changing workforce, and changing organizational needs. Strategic planning in support organizations should include the largest number of staff possible. Although the manager may be tempted to gather a few people together to develop the plan (drawing upon a business model for strategic planning), it is important to develop an understanding and commitment to change among the staff members by involving them in creating the strategic plan.

The strategic planning process should be facilitated by a neutral party. The facilitator's role is to keep the process moving. The facilitator should not attempt to influence the content of the strategic plan but should stick to helping the planning team by leading them through the process steps and ensuring that all planning team members are participating.

PREWORK

In many cases, it is a good idea to preface the strategic planning meeting by providing participants with data they may need to digest before they become engaged in the planning process. For example, there may be important budgetary information that participants should see and consider prior to the session. There might be feedback from a variety of surveys, self-assessment studies, or external reviews that people need time to study prior to the meeting. If this type of information is shared, it is essential that all participants are able to see the same information before the meeting.

START WITH SOME REFLECTION

The strategic planning process should begin with a bit of reflection. Although everyone may want to jump in and start discussing the future, there is great value in some reflection about the past and the present circumstances that may profoundly influence the future direction of the organization. This time of reflection will provide the organization's leadership with an opportunity to share information that may provide a compelling case for change. It gives people an opportunity to let reality sink in a bit and prepares them to think about the need for change within their organization that may well impact their everyday lives.

The reflection for the strategic planning process could be generated from a self-assessment process using feedback from stakeholders. By using either a short form for self-assessment or a more detailed evaluation using the framework of a national standard for quality in education, the strategic planning team can gain valuable insights into the institutional issues that need to be addressed in the strategic plan. The findings from a self-assessment can be presented to the strategic planning team prior to their initial meeting or as part of the process of reflection when the team is assembled.

There are three tools that are widely used to stimulate reflection in preparation for the strategic plan. *Timelines* are used to create a common understanding of the history of the organization. A *proud and sorry* exercise enables a planning team to acknowledge past actions that were high points and low points in the organization's history.[4] A *SWOT analysis* permits the organization to review its current strengths, weaknesses, opportunities, and threats. Each of these tools creates an opportunity to build a common understanding of events that are now impacting the organization. They build a more level playing field between new and old members of the group and provide everyone with a similar perspective

	Strong state economy	Slower state economy		
	New building		Hiring freeze	New hires
Separate Chancellor	Interim	Apple II	Internet	
For Law Center	Chancellor	Computers	Lap Tops	

1960s	1970s	1980s	1990s	2000

Figure 5.1 Paul Herbert Law Center Timeline

concerning factual information that must be considered in developing a vision of what the organization needs to become.

In the *timeline* exercise, the group collectively builds a history of the organization, going back as far as the memory of the person with the longest history in the group. The timeline is drawn on flip chart pages that may stretch across a wall in the room where the planning team is meeting. This sometimes starts with a senior faculty or staff member who takes a few minutes to describe what the department, college, or group was like forty years ago. The entire group needs to hear about some of the personalities, the technology that was employed, and other major events or conditions that defined that time. This is important validation for the senior members of the group and can provide valuable insights for newer people of the group. Information for the timeline is drawn from all the group members and continues right up to the present. Figure 5.1 is an example drawn from a timeline developed by the faculty in the Law School at Louisiana State University as an initial exercise in their strategic planning process in 2003.

After the timeline exercise is complete, it is beneficial to leave it on the wall during the rest of the planning process. Ask participants to ponder the timeline and to identify any trends or issues that will be carried into the future.

The *proud and sorry* exercise requires everyone in the group to reflect on the information in the timeline exercise. People are then asked to identify things about their organization's past that they are proud of and the things they are sorry about. These should be written on a list that will be posted on a wall throughout the rest of the planning process. This is a powerful exercise that allows people to acknowledge the positive things that have happened in their department or college. It also allows a time for healing regarding some of the hurtful moments people have experienced. Many institutions need an opportunity for people to acknowledge historical wrongs that have been committed. The proud and sorry exercise may not be needed for all groups in strategic planning, but in some cases it is a necessary and helpful step.

The *SWOT analysis* is widely used in business and educational strategic planning. Members of the planning team list the strengths (S) of the organization, the weaknesses (W), the opportunities (O), and the threats (T). Thoughtful leaders will prepare the planning team for this step by providing some background data. The data will help the planning team understand what the leader may know in terms of problem areas and opportunities. People may be in denial that problems exist, so some background data will help people see their situation from a different perspective. It should be noted that when people list their strengths, they often paint with a broad brush. A major strength, such as quality of the faculty, may just take up one line on a page. When people list their weaknesses, they often use a fine brush, so the number of weaknesses identified may outnumber the strengths, but it is important to consider the amount of detail that people may have used regarding the weaknesses.

It is usually a good idea to list strengths, weaknesses, threats, and then to end on opportunities. If the group ends the exercise on threats, it can be discouraging. Strive to end on an upbeat by considering the opportunities. The SWOT analysis is another tool used to build a common perspective about the current status of the organization. It will provide useful information when the planning team moves on to consider the future. The objective of these reflective exercises is to create a common understanding of the need for change.

This is also the time to review important data that will further help create a level playing field within the planning group. Feedback from climate surveys or from outcome surveys would be valuable for a planning team to review. Budgetary information or comparative data from similar institutions can also be important at this stage.

CREATE A VISION

Once the planning team has spent some time in serious reflection, the stage is set for creating a vision of what the team would like to see the organization become in five to ten years. In the past, some institutions have been successful with longer range strategic plans, but technical and social change often makes this impractical and unadvisable.

The facilitator can help the group members create a vision by leading them through a vision creation exercise. In this exercise, the facilitator invites the participants to imagine that they are gathered together five, seven, or ten years in the future. They are gathered together in order to receive some type of reward or recognition for being the best unit of their type. (The facilitator must work with the chair of the team ahead of time to define what the recognition should be so that it will be credible and meaningful to the team members.) The facilitator asks the group members to imagine they are in the future and are about to receive this reward, then asks the members to describe this future state. It is important to suggest that everyone may not agree on the future state. They do not have to have a consensus at this point. They only need to share their dreams, their hopes, and their aspirations for the organization. The facilitator collects these descriptions of the future state of the organization on easel pages that are posted where everyone in the group can see them.

This is a very dynamic, exciting process. Participants usually get excited about sharing their vision, and one person's comments generally stimulate other comments from the group. It is important at this stage that the facilitator not allow participants to begin to critique the vision. There does not have to be 100 percent unanimous agreement about the elements of the vision of the future. That agreement will take shape when people start talking about actions.

LOOK BACK FROM THE FUTURE

Once the group members have shared their ideas about a desirable future state for their organization, they need to quickly move on to discussing how this future state was achieved. Ask the group members to imagine that they are still in the future, some seven to ten years from now. They have described the future state for which they are about to receive a reward or recognition. Suggest to them that, as part of the awards ceremony, they must describe the major actions they took that moved them from where they were seven or ten years ago to achieve this award-winning future state. Ask the group members to look back and describe what it was they had to do to move from where they were to where they imagine themselves to be in the future. As people share their ideas, write them on an easel page in large letters so everyone can see the emerging idea. Continue this exercise until all the ideas have been exhausted from the group.

Ask the group to reflect on the actions to see if anything has been left out. For each feature of a potential future state, there should be at least one action that described what the members did to move in that direction.

An organization cannot charge off and work on forty or fifty actions simultaneously and expect to have much success. It is essential to prioritize the list of potential actions to determine which actions are the ones that generate the most commitment and enthusiasm from the participants.

With a large group of people, this means using some form of nominal group technique.[5]

First, ask the participants to review the list of actions to see if any are duplicates or may convey the same idea with slightly different wording. Get the group to identify what ideas should be combined. Then count the total number of possible actions and divide by three to determine how many choices each participant will have. If there are sixty possible actions, then each participant will be allowed to select the twenty that he or she think are most important to take in order to move the organization in the direction it needs to go. Participants usually enjoy being given the appropriate number of colored adhesive dots (used in offices to code file folders) and being asked to place one dot by each of their top choices. It is important to instruct people not to place more than one dot by each of their top selections. People tend to enjoy this activity for several reasons. First, it allows them to get up and do something after sitting in a meeting. Second, it allows the group to see the pattern that has emerged. The areas of strong consensus can quickly be seen by the whole group.

Nominal group technique offers several advantages for developing a consensus. First is that it can be a rapid process. No one is allowed to block a particular option by arguing extensively against it. Second, people can see that their own ideas are either supported or ignored by the group as a whole. In one session, a faculty member gave a passionate speech regarding his idea, which then only received one dot. He quickly learned that his colleagues did not share his perspective. Third, it allows the group to easily see the areas where there is a strong consensus in terms of what actions should be taken.

Identify the hypothetical actions that were selected by at least half the participants as being the active list of actions, and rank this short list of actions based on the number of times each was selected. There may actually be a few actions that everyone in the group chose. These are the set of unanimous actions that must be included in the action plan. The rest of the items on the short list are about to become the consensus actions. To achieve a consensus on these items, it is necessary to ask the participants if anyone is absolutely opposed to an item on the short list. This is not asking the participants to endorse the action but to be certain that none of the actions would be impossible for some member of the group to live with.

It is important to point out to the participants that, although they may have generated a lengthy list of potential actions, no organization can effectively go out and do forty or fifty things at once. The group members need to concentrate on the most important actions they can take over the next two to three years that will have the most impact in terms of where the organization will be in seven to ten years. As the highest priority items are completed, they can certainly work their way further down the list.

DEVELOP ACTION PLANS

Once the group has identified the key actions that need to occur to move the organization in the desired direction, the group needs to move on to developing specific action plans. The development of action plans immediately causes the planning team to confront two issues. First, the organization cannot do everything at once. While some initiatives can be launched in the first year of the plan, others will have to wait until the second and third year. Second, the sooner an initiative is launched, the sooner it will begin to impact the long-term condition of the organization. As in changing the direction of a ship, the sooner you begin to steer in a new direction, the sooner you will achieve gradual, long-term change.

Although an organization's strategic plan may seek to look seven or more years into the future, the plan is typically useful for only about three years before it should be seriously revised and updated. Therefore, the planning horizon for action plans should not greatly exceed three years. Four years should be the outside limit for action plans.

Strategic planning is like driving across the country at night. The ultimate destination (the vision of what the organization is to become) may be a great distance away, but you must be careful not to overdrive your headlights by planning actions that are more than three years in the future.

Effective action plans are often developed by breaking the strategic planning team into subgroups. In some cases, a subgroup may bring in people who were not part of the overall strategic planning process in order to gain insight and expertise in a specific area, such as the use of technology in classrooms or in planning the development of Web-based classes. Many organizations will identify someone to serve as the leader for each of the subgroups and will establish a due date by which the subgroup is to develop its action plan.

The objective of creating action plans is to define what specific steps will occur to implement a key strategic action, to define who will be responsible for each step, and to define a time frame for the completion of each step. A major action plan may include numerous steps with completion dates (sometimes called milestones) defined for each step. In some

Activity	Primary Individual	Timetable
Enhance contact with Undergraduate majors:		
a. Evaluate advising via e-mail poll	Pawley	Implement in Fall 1997 after advising
b. Develop/maintain regular e-mail contact with majors	Raffetto	First contact in Spring 1997
c. Prepare and distribute flyer about zoology major to all students in all courses.	Raffetto	Spring 1997 distribution
Develop workable data base of majors	Kuhl	May 1997

Figure 5.2   Action Plan

cases, it is beneficial to define points in time when progress on the implementation of a plan will be formally reviewed. It may also be beneficial to clarify or define the endpoint for an action plan. How will you know you have reached your destination? At what point will you declare victory and celebrate?

Figure 5.2 is an example of an action plan from the Department of Zoology at the University of Wisconsin–Madison.[6]

USING THE STRATEGIC PLAN

Some organizations fail in their strategic planning process after they have developed an exciting plan because they place the new plan on a shelf and do not use it on a regular basis. Imagine the frustration and cynicism that then develops among the people who gave their time and energy to develop a strategic plan as the plan begins to gather dust. In the day-to-day rush of events, however, the strategic plan can become ignored. People may be rewarded for focusing on the latest crisis rather than for steering the organization by following up on the actions in the strategic plan.

The strategic plan needs to become the organization's mantra. It should reverberate throughout the organization like a regular drumbeat. The dean, department chair, or director that "owns" the plan should regularly

Responsibility	Project Description	January – March	April - June	July - September	October – December
BE/JA	Increase the number of computers in the labs to 40	▓	▓	▓	▓
BE/JA	Purchase and install 7 new workstations	▓			
JA/BE	Install workstations in small lab		▓		
JA	Prepare for Testing		▓		
BE/JA	Purchase additional computers			▓	
JA	Install new computers				▓

Figure 5.3   Gantt Chart from Lowery Learning Resource Center

use the plan in meetings to review progress on strategic actions. A review of strategic actions should be a regular action item in all staff meetings.

Leaders can emphasize the attention given to the plan by developing Gantt charts to track progress on the action plans.[7] Gantt, a pioneer in the field of engineering (who lectured at Stevens, Columbia, Harvard, and Yale), developed these charts to allow people to visually track the progress on complex projects in which there are multiple steps. Figure 5.3 is a Gantt chart used at the Lowery Learning Resource Center in the College of Nursing at The University of Alabama. The chart enables the center's director and the dean to track multiple improvement projects occurring within the center.

As an organization begins to implement the action plans in its strategic plan, it will often encounter "the fog of war." This term emerged from the eighteenth- and nineteenth-century military leaders who observed that once troops or ships engaged in action, it was difficult to tell what was happening due to all the smoke from guns and dust from cavalry. Without a Gantt chart, it can be difficult to determine if an organization is actually making progress on the action plans because of the smoke and dust that arises from the day-to-day work on any campus. Most organizations will encounter new issues or problems that were unforeseen during the planning. These issues may not change the vision, but they may impact the rate at which the organization can focus resources on accomplishing the action steps. Unforeseen declines in revenue, unanticipated expenses and problems with facilities, or even the unexpected illness or move of a key contributor may require due dates or action plans to slip. This slippage can be discouraging, but a visual tracking tool, such as the Gantt chart, permits the organization to clearly redefine the new completion dates and helps to keep everyone apprised of the change.

Although only a few days may be spent in developing the strategic plan, the implementation may involve years of work. People from all parts of the campus may be involved in implementing the plan, so it is wise to ensure that these diverse groups have had a voice in the planning process. Those who create tend to support.

REVISITING THE STRATEGIC PLAN

The mission of an organization can last for centuries, however, the vision that supports the mission must be renewed every three to five years in order to stay abreast of changing world conditions. In the early 1900s, universities would develop a fifty-year strategic plan. It would take twenty-five years to accomplish all the key actions in the fifty-year plan. Today, with changing technology, changing institutional leadership, variation in state funding, changing federal initiatives, changing student demographics, and fluctuating national and regional economies, an institution of higher education cannot afford to conduct strategic planning on a twenty-five- to fifty-year cycle.

A three- to five-year strategic planning cycle allows the higher education institution to maintain a fresh vision and to keep developing new actions and initiatives that will help the institution achieve its vision. It will be difficult to gain commitment from faculty and staff if past strategic planning processes were drawn-out, laborious processes that exhausted participants and only produced a document that was promptly ignored by everyone.

In the 1980s, a popular book about management fads suggested that successful organizations should use a process of ready, fire, aim for planning.[8] The thought was that organizations can waste valuable time through excessive planning and that it is often better to get out and do something rather than sit around planning. The stakes are too high in higher education to adopt this model, and many corporations that tried it have done poorly. One may even argue that a great many expensive ventures into Web-based businesses and Web-based classes fit the ready, fire, aim model of planning. The proper approach is ready, aim, fire. The secret for success is to aim quickly and aim well.

Effective leaders embrace the concept of strategic planning and recognize there is a natural cycle for planning and a natural need to develop a new strategic plan every three to five years. The actual moment to revisit the cycle and develop a new plan can be triggered by a variety of circumstances, such as the completion of most of the action items in a plan, a change in leadership, a major change in technology, or a significant new demand, such as the opening of a new business in the school's region or the emergence of a new field, such as e-commerce.

If the winds of change are strong, do not refuse to revisit the strategic plan simply because the institution has only partially implemented the current plan. The long-term destination may remain the same, but there may be a need to develop a strategy to steer around a hurricane or to use a new wind to your strategic advantage.

PROBLEMS WITH MISSION STATEMENTS

Many academic and administrative groups have weak mission statements. It may not be worth the effort to change a poor mission statement if it means slowing down the development of a strategic plan that is urgently needed. However, in some instances, the timing may be right to refine a group's mission statement.

How does one distinguish an inspiring mission statement from a dull one? Dull, ineffective mission statements simply define or state what the organization does. We teach students. We feed students. We admit students.

Exciting mission statements define what the organization accomplishes. It is worthwhile to spend some time defining the end result that justifies all of the work and compels people to devote their lives to this type of work. The real accomplishment may be to add value to the community, to explore and create new knowledge, to prepare leaders for the future, or to solve social or economic problems. These are missions that motivate people.

Examine your institution's mission statement and ask if it inspires people and excites them about coming to the campus. Will the mission statement excite people about serving on your board of advisors? Will it attract students to your institution? If your mission statement generates a yawn, it probably focuses on what the institution does and not on what it accomplishes.

STRATEGIC PLANNING WITH A UNIVERSITY SYSTEM

The Troy State University System in Alabama wanted to develop a strategic plan for the entire system, made up of a primary campus in Troy, a campus in Montgomery, and campuses in Dothan and Phoenix City, Alabama. They chose a planning model that was based on the future search methodology.

The president of the Troy-Montgomery campus led a small team that organized the strategic planning process. Their first step was to identify a planning team that represented the diverse interests of faculty and staff on the multiple campuses. A team of over eighty people was assembled at a state park meeting facility for a one-and a-half-day planning session that opened with welcoming remarks by the chancellor.

The planning activity began with a timeline exercise that involved the whole team in identifying significant events, people, practices, and changes in the Troy State University System over the previous thirty years. This helped create a level playing field among the new faculty and staff and those who had worked in the system for decades. It also helped the whole group appreciate how much the system had changed over the decades and created a sense that this type of change is normal.

The timeline exercise was followed by a panel discussion featuring the presidents of each of the campuses. The presidents had prepared a list of what they saw as the strengths, weaknesses, opportunities, and threats for the Troy State University System. They were very open in their comments, and the floor was open for participants to ask questions and offer additional perspectives.

The entire gathering then broke into five smaller groups to spend an hour creating lists of the things they were proud of and the things they were sorry about concerning their system. Each small group shared its lists with the large group, and people were interested to see the similarities among the lists. This exercise allowed everyone in the group to have a voice and for everyone to hear the summary of all the groups.

The group then broke for some "soak time," where people could enjoy the park facilities, engage in discussions, and reflect on what they had heard. They reconvened the next morning. Participants were again divided into small groups. Each group identified ideas and opportunities for improvement in three strategic areas: academic programs, student and administrative services, and community development. (These categories were preselected by the small team that planned the agenda for the strategic planning meeting.) Each group prepared a short presentation that was given when the entire group reconvened.

The entire group heard the recommendations from all the teams. A list was compiled as each team identified issues and opportunities in the three strategic areas. Major themes were identified in each strategic area. For example, in the area of student and administrative services, the small groups identified ideas and needs that could be grouped together in the categories of reviewing work processes, standardizing processes and terminology across campuses, expanding the use of Web-based resources, and training staff to take ownership for personally resolving problems that students have. No one knew what these categories would be. They emerged as each small group reported on its discussions. Teams were then identified to develop action plans after the planning conference to turn the ideas into actions.

This is an excellent example of how strategic planning leads the organization into quality improvement. The discussion among faculty and staff identified the need to improve work processes and to provide better training to staff.

STRATEGIC PLANNING WITH A UNIVERSITY

The University of Iowa has completed several five-year planning cycles. Like many universities, Iowa's plan identifies a relatively small number of overall goals. In the two most recent plans, Iowa has strengthened the plan by identifying strategic indicators to measure its progress in each of the overall goals. For a strategic plan with seven overall goals, Iowa developed thirty-five areas to measure to determine the university's progress toward the overall goals. In each of these thirty-five areas, targets were established to be achieved within five years, based on input from a variety of stakeholders.

For example, Goal Four concerns "Distinguished Research and Scholarship." In this area, Iowa will measure external research funding, intellectual property disclosures, and library rankings.

Iowa's president-emeritus, Dr. Mary Sue Coleman, has observed that strategic planning, combined with strategic indicators and performance goals, provide many advantages. This approach certainly enhanced communications with all stakeholder groups, both inside and outside the campus. By understanding the strategic goals, employees have been able to enact changes at their own levels in the organization to support the strategic goals.[9]

STRATEGIC PLANNING WITH A COLLEGE

The School of Social Work at The University of Alabama was undergoing a transition. The fourth dean of the school was stepping down after many successful years. She had led the school through the development and completion of a strategic plan six years earlier. Her successor was a professor from the faculty of the school who had spent the previous two years in an executive role in the provost's office.

The incoming dean recognized the need for a strategic planning process that would acknowledge the school's success, energize the faculty to take on new challenges, and position the school well for reaccreditation that was due within eighteen months.

The dean coordinated a series of half-day sessions with the faculty, meeting in the student union building across campus. These sessions began with a timeline exercise that reconstructed the history of the school. This was beneficial for the newer faculty and for the few faculty members who had been at the school since its beginnings in the late 1960s. The timeline helped the faculty see how the schools' role had changed within the state, within the campus, and within the field of social work.

The timeline exercise was followed by a good deal of reflection over the strengths, weaknesses, threats, and opportunities. The faculty filled up pages of easel pads with their observations. It was the first time in many years that they had reflected on how far they had come in the previous years and their sense of frustration regarding all that they yet needed to do.

After reflection regarding strengths, weaknesses, threats, and opportunities, the faculty members engaged in a visioning exercise to describe where they would like to see the department in seven years. This discussion brought out many differences in vision among the faculty. Some members wanted the department to continue its focus on research. Others wanted the department members to engage in discussion regarding the ideological foundations of their teaching. Some wanted the department to take a more activist approach in advocating changes in social policies in the region.

Through nominal group technique and through a good deal of discussion, the faculty was able to work out a strategic plan that would address its varied interests. The members established common ground in their desire for research and advocacy. They also agreed on several actions that focused on improving academic programs and conditions for graduate students.

STRATEGIC PLANNING WITH A COMMUNITY COLLEGE

Western Wisconsin Technical College (WWTC) has refined its strategic planning process to combine strategic challenges, strategic priorities, short- and long-term objectives, performance measures, a baseline for these measures, five-year targets, comparative data, and results data.[10]

WWTC's current strategic plan starts with strategic challenges, such as providing a high-quality technical education with limited resources. A strategic priority for meeting this challenge is to "maintain a stable enrollment by offering a comprehensive, cost-effective mix of programs and services that reflect the dynamic needs of the district" that WWTC serves.[11] Expanding alternative delivery options becomes both a short-term and long-term objective. Increasing enrollment and maintaining fiscal responsibility to taxpayers are both long-term objectives. Performance measures are established for each objective. WWTC's FY 2000 enrollment of 21,028 students serves as a baseline. The target for 2005–2006 is 24,000 students.

Each strategic priority at WWTC is summarized by a key factor, such as enrollment, retention, student learning, student satisfaction, and stakeholder satisfaction. Each factor has measures that are often linked to national comparative data.

STRATEGIC PLANNING WITH AN ACADEMIC DEPARTMENT

The Art and Design Department is the largest academic program at the University of Wisconsin–Stout, with 850 majors enrolled in this program. Because of continued growth and the addition of new faculty to the department, the department chair felt that the timing was right for developing a new strategic plan for the department.

All the faculty members and the departmental secretary met on a Thursday and Friday early in the semester at a restaurant and conference facility that was about thirty minutes away from the campus.

Prior to the meeting, the faculty received budgetary information about the department, along with information on enrollment trends, so that all faculty members would have a common understanding about the important financial issues facing the department.

The strategic planning session began with a timeline exercise. The history of the department, going back twenty-five years, was reconstructed on pages that filled a wall in the conference facility. A great deal of valuable information was shared with the newer faculty members, while the older faculty members had the opportunity to reflect on the many challenges and changes they had weathered over the years.

The timeline exercise was followed by a SWOT analysis in which the faculty members examined their enrollment figures, their budgets, their staffing levels, their facilities, and the reputation of their department with employers who hire their graduates. Faculty members were encouraged to share their perspectives without having to reach any consensus on whether everyone would agree with a faculty member's specific observation. One professor might consider a facility to be a weakness, while another might see it as a strength, and this difference of perspective was encouraged to help everyone better understand how the department was viewed in different ways.

After some realistic assessment of their strengths, weaknesses, opportunities, and threats, the faculty members developed a vision of what the department might become over the next seven years. They developed some exciting ideas in their vision but also stayed within the realm of reason. The visioning exercise again allowed individual faculty members to express differing views. There was no drive to gain consensus on the vision. Instead, the visioning exercise was another opportunity to allow faculty members to learn more from each other regarding how they each viewed the possible future of the department.

Based on their discussion of a vision of what the department might become, the faculty members discussed the types of actions that would need to occur in order to move the department in the general direction they would like to see it go. They developed a list of possible actions and narrowed the list down to a vital few, through nominal group technique, to develop a list of their top ten action areas.

By using nominal group technique, the faculty developed a list that identified the areas of strongest consensus among the faculty. No one won or lost by having a vote. Every faculty member (and the departmental secretary) had an equal voice in the decision-making process, and everyone had issues they supported show up on the list of the top actions.

Faculty chose to focus on establishing an improved process to review curriculum, creating a national juried exhibition for student work, and establishment of a Master of Fine Arts program in the College of Arts and Sciences. Within the first year, the faculty had made significant progress on all three strategic goals and had restructured the department's committee system and revised the department's by-laws regarding personnel issues.

STRATEGIC PLANNING WITH A SUPPORT ORGANIZATION

The new director of the University of Georgia press believed that the press was in need of a new vision and strategic plan to energize the organization. The director could compare the press's performance against other scholarly publishers and could see considerable room for improvement. Some of the staff members at the press had been there for many years and considered the present state of affairs to be normal. Others were eager to develop new products and approaches to marketing their books.

The director launched a strategic planning process. She first gathered pertinent comparative data regarding the performance of the press and the performance of other scholarly presses. Having collected the evidence that would present the need for change, she scheduled an all-day planning off-site with all of the staff.

The director saw that it was important to involve everyone at the press in the strategic planning process, because the press needed to change and everyone was going to have to be convinced of the need for change before it change could effectively occur. She also recognized the need to get the staff members out of their offices for a day, where they would not be interrupted by the busy day-to-day work of working with authors and preparing manuscripts and illustrations.

The strategic planning off-site began with a timeline exercise. Long-time employees enjoyed relating the ups and downs of the press over the previous twenty-five years as it moved from an old location to new facilities, adapted new technology, and experienced a variety of leaders. Newer employees discovered that their colleagues had overcome some very interesting challenges.

The timeline exercise was followed by a SWOT analysis. The group discussed the relative strengths, weaknesses, opportunities, and threats facing the press. At this time, the director shared the comparative performance data so all the staff members could see how they compared with other presses. Staff members offered many perspectives and learned a great deal about how others in the organization saw their situation.

The staff members then participated in a visioning exercise. They imagined that it was seven years into the future and they were assembled to receive an award for excellence in the field of scholarly publication. They created a vision in which they would maintain their reputation for high-quality scholarly books but would also increase the number of titles produced each year.

With this vision in place, the staff members brainstormed a list of actions they would have had to have taken over the seven-year period to obtain their desired future state. They listed over twenty possible areas for change in their organization. After they had developed an exhaustive list of ideas, the staff members prioritized the actions, using a nominal group method, resulting in seven key strategic areas on which everyone agreed they needed to focus.

Staff then devoted the afternoon to developing action plans for each of the seven strategic areas. The staff divided into four teams that discussed the top four strategic areas and developed an action plan for each one. The teams members then reported their plans to the entire group for a critique. Team members then modified their plans to incorporate ideas from the critique. New teams were then formed to develop plans for the final three areas, and those plans were also critiqued by the whole group and modified by the teams.

SUMMARY

Although continuous improvement efforts may start by working on immediate problems on a campus, long-term improvement depends on the use of a systematic approach to self-assessment and the development of strategic plans in a manner that is suitable for the academic environment. Using a traditional corporate model of strategic planning often fails to provide appropriate participation from faculty and staff in the higher education setting. An alternative, "future search" model creates a highly participative approach that generates faculty commitment to strategic plans. Academic leaders can obtain ideas for continuous improvement and strategic planning through a variety of methods. One effective method is through benchmarking of other academic, or even nonacademic, organizations that have evidenced excellence that other institutions would like to emulate.

NOTES

1. University of Wisconsin–Stout, *Application for the Malcolm Baldrige National Quality Award, 2001.*

2. Charles Sorensen and Diane Moen, "Winning the Baldrige National Quality Award," in *Pursuing Excellence in Higher Education* (San Francisco: Jossey-Bass, 2004).

3. Marvin Weisbord, *Developing Common Ground* (San Francisco: Barrett-Kohler Press, 1992).

4. Ibid.

5. Donald C. Moseley, "Nominal Grouping as an Organizational Development Intervention Technique," *Training and Development Journal* (March 1974): 30–37.

6. Warren Porter and Kathleen Paris, "Creating a Strategic Plan," Department of Zoology, The University of Wisconsin–Madison, 1998.

7. Henry Gantt, *Industrial Leadership* (New Haven, CT: Yale University Press, 1916).

8. Thomas J. Peters and Robert H. Waterman, *In Search of Excellence* (New York: Warner Books, 1982).

9. Mary Sue Coleman, "Implementing a Strategic Plan Using Indicators and Targets," in *Pursuing Excellence in Higher Education* (San Francisco: Jossey-Bass, 2004).

10. Lee Rasch, "Quality . . . The Western Way," NCCI Conference, 2002.

11. Ibid.

CHAPTER

Benchmarking in the
Academic Environment

A definite benefit of the benchmarking studies in higher education is the introspection it requires—institutions are forced to
study their own processes, collect information, and raise questions
about the efficiency of current processes and systems in place.
—Susan Engelkemeyer

The term *benchmarking* has a very different meaning within the continuous improvement field compared with how the term has traditionally been used in academic settings. In academe, schools benchmark themselves against other similar institutions to see if they are
performing in a similar way. If a school is similar to its peer institutions,
then the administration usually accepts this as a validation of its processes.
For example, if students complain about not being able to understand a
math instructor at a school, the school may benchmark similar institutions to find out if their students have the same complaints. If they find
that their peer institutions are receiving similar complaints, then these
complaints are categorized as normal and the problem is explained away
as just being a problem that all schools must live with. In academe,
benchmarking has often meant looking at how other schools are doing
and, if our peers have the same problems, then we are all okay.

The concept of benchmarking in the continuous improvement field
emerges from a different cultural tradition. When Japan opened its borders to Europeans in the late 1800s, the Japanese sent observers to Eu-
rope and America to identify the best practices in government, education,

and economics. The Japanese adopted the most successful components of Western government, commerce, and education from a variety of countries. This practice continued into the twentieth century and contributed to Japan's economic success in the post-war era. When Xerox Corporation lost over half of its market share to the Japanese in the 1970s, Fuji Xerox president Yataro Kobayashi encouraged his American counterparts to compare U.S. operations to Japanese operations. A landmark comparison in 1979 led Xerox to develop a continuous process of identifying best practices and adopting them into its own culture and operations, which they called *benchmarking*.[1]

In the continuous improvement field, benchmarking means finding out who is the best in an area, studying how they work, and adopting the best practices that are suitable to your own organization. This does not mean making an uncritical, blind adoption of another organization's policies and practices. The benchmarking organization observes best practices from the perspective of looking for new ideas that will fit within its organizational context.

When Binghamton University began its quality initiative, for example, it began by benchmarking Penn State, Rutgers, and Villanova to identify effective practices and lessons learned from those institutions.

BENCHMARKING PROMPTS

There are a variety of ways to naturally step into the benchmarking process. A self-assessment, using a Baldrige criteria or some other state or association criteria, may help an institution identify areas in need of improvement. Benchmarking is often a logical first step to improve a particular function.

The strategic planning process helps institutions identify a key set of high priority areas to work on. As action plans are developed for the key areas, benchmarking may be the logical first step. Likewise, an institution that has used stakeholder surveys may find low satisfaction in a particular area and might choose benchmarking as the first step in discovering how a problem area can be improved. In reviewing the institution's set of performance indicators, a president, dean, or provost might see a worsening trend and decide to find an institution with an improving trend and learn what it is doing that is different. Benchmarking can also be stimulated when people review national comparative data, such as the University of Delaware's comparative study, comparative data from groups such as the National Collegiate Athletic Association, and information from professional organizations, such as the National Association for College and University Business Officers (NACUBO). Even questionable comparative data, such as the *U.S. News & World Report's* school rankings might stimulate benchmarking of other institutions.

TYPES OF BENCHMARKING

Robert Camp identified four classifications of benchmarking that all fit within the context of higher education.[2]

1. *Internal benchmarking* consists of comparative study of data or processes within an institution. The comparative analysis of practices related to the use of technology in the classroom on a single campus, for example, may reveal effective practices that can be promoted across the campus.

2. *Competitive benchmarking* promotes the comparison of information about processes between institutions. This type of benchmarking is often sponsored by neutral professional associations but may be hampered by differences in definition of work processes between institutions. The University of Delaware's comparative study of academic programs and the National Association of College and University Business Officers' comparative study of administrative costs are prime examples of competitive benchmarking. Competitive benchmarking can be a valuable tool for comparisons among campuses within a university system.

3. *Functional benchmarking* compares process performance in diverse settings. Food court operations in a student center, for example, can be compared with similar operations in a shopping mall. Research practices on a campus can be compared with research practices at national laboratories and in the corporate setting.

4. *Best in Class* benchmarking focuses on finding out who has the exceptional performance in a particular area, studying their methods, and adopting their processes, where possible.

The challenge for "Best in Class" benchmarking is to aggressively seek out examples of other institutions that are really doing a remarkable job. Institutions must overcome a great deal of inertia and active resistance by those with a vested interest in maintaining the status quo to effectively utilize benchmarking.

"HOW DID YOU COOK THE DATA?"

One lesson learned about benchmarking other institutions came several years ago in researching issues related to six-year graduation rates. A flagship state university in one state had a significantly higher six-year graduation rate than many other public universities. A staff member called this other school and asked what it had done to achieve this success. The representative from the other school appreciated the way the question was posed. He said that he gets a couple of calls every year on this subject, and that people always ask him, "How did your school cook the data?" The data were accurate, he said, and he always resented the way the question was asked, so he rarely shared any new ideas with callers. Because the caller had asked the right question, he proceeded to share a half-dozen innovations that had slowly enabled his school to improve its six-year graduation rate.

Another lesson learned has been to look beyond our national borders. Alabama needed to make a step change in its ability to allow students to enroll in courses on-line, to conduct on-line degree audits, and to use a computer system to help students schedule their classes. The Registrar's office conducted a benchmarking effort and determined that the best system was developed and deployed in Canada.

Benchmarking can be used to improve academic programs, support services, and a wide range of campus issues. Binghamton University used benchmarking to address the issue of alcohol and drug use among students. Binghamton staff traveled to Penn State and to the University of Virginia to study their methods for addressing these concerns and then developed Binghamton's "Late Nite" program to offer an alternate venue for student activities.

The University of California–Berkeley conducted a major benchmarking study of continuous improvement in higher education before launching their CI initiative in 1999. UC–Berkeley studied continuous improvement activities at Harvard, Penn State, University of Texas at Austin, Purdue, University of Wisconsin–Madison, Arizona State University, and Rutgers.

Through analysis of several approaches, the UC–Berkeley team recommended the establishment of an office reporting to the chancellor for continuous improvement, establishment of a partnership with Hewlett-Packard, and the development and use of planning and process improvement tools across the campus.[3]

SYSTEMATIC BENCHMARKING

Benchmarking should be a continuous process for an academic institution, not a one-time event. The process engages an institution in continuous learning by reflection on the factors that are critical for its success, comparison of the institution's performance to those that are best-in-class, and development of the appropriate institutional strategies for improvement. Through benchmarking, colleges and universities allow themselves to evaluate their status and to envision where they need to be to become excellent.

There are six phases in the benchmarking process:

1. Determining what to benchmark;
2. Organizing the benchmarking team;
3. Determining whom to benchmark;
4. Collecting data from other organizations;
5. Analyzing the data;
6. Implementing improvements; and
7. Recalibrating the institution.

Step One: The institution needs to determine what work processes and what results are vital for the success of the organization. What activities will ensure successful competitive performance when students, parents, corporations, government agencies, and grant-giving organizations decide which schools they will support? The institution must think in terms of the "things that must go right" for the school to flourish.

It is important for the institution to identify its distinctive competencies—those unique strengths that provide a competitive advantage and are demonstrably different in the eyes of the stakeholders. The critical success factors should be prioritized so that the most important issues are addressed first. As benchmarking is adopted as a continuous process, all the items on the list of critical success factors will eventually be addressed, but you must start somewhere, and no institution can do everything at once; so, prioritize.

Step Two: Organize a team to conduct a specific benchmarking activity. The team should begin by collecting some internal data to define how well the process currently performs, and/or how the results currently look. It is important to understand the strengths and weaknesses of the internal process before attempting to identify external benchmarks.

Step Three: Determine whom to benchmark. Identifying the organization that is best in class may take some time. Check with your peers in professional societies to determine who has a reputation for a strong program in the area you want to benchmark. Most benchmarking in higher education will be comparisons with other colleges and universities, but do not overlook the possibility of benchmarking a business that has a best practice in areas such as human resource management, information management, maintenance, and purchasing. Comparative data are available through national surveys conducted by the University of Delaware, The Pew Charitable Trusts, the Carnegie Foundation for the Advancement of Teaching, and the National Association of College and University Business Officers (NACUBO). It may be difficult to admit, but sometimes the best school to benchmark is the one that is your greatest rival. Do not be reluctant to benchmark against the school that is your greatest competitor for students, research grants, faculty, and even in athletics. Keep an eye out in education journals for information that may lead you to discover that another institution has made significant advances in a particular area that may have moved them to become best in class.

Also, be sure to consider internal benchmarking. A college that is part of a university may have a problem with developing effective relations with alumni. Another college on the same campus may be one of the best in the region in effective alumni relations. A lot could be learned through a visit across the campus.

Step Four: Collect the data. Obtaining comparative figures between the best-in-class organization and your own institution is the bottom line in benchmarking. Whether the data are qualitative or quantitative, they must be compared with your own baseline data to fully understand the differences. Data collection can be conducted through telephone calls, visits to other campuses, or at professional society meetings. Biology faculty members who want to improve some aspect of their program might find the information concerning a best-in-class program at a national conference.

Step Five: Analyze the data. Data analyses begin by determining the actual gap between your organization's performance and the best-in-class organization. How much of a gap actually exists? Then identify the policies, philosophies, or actions that have enabled the best-in-class organization to achieve its higher level of performance. What has it done that is different from everyone else? Perhaps it has followed the same steps as other schools but has added a special emphasis or some unique feature. What is it?

Data analyses should lead the benchmarking team to develop new strategies, or improvements on current strategies, that will enable the organization to rise to the level of the best in class. In most cases, this is simply not a matter of spending more money. In fact, some best-in-class organizations may be spending less money than their peers, but they are spending it more wisely. In some cases, benchmarking is performed when your organization is at ground zero, such as launching a quality initiative. In these situations, the benchmarking campus examines what others are doing that appears effective and takes the best ideas that they believe will fit into their campus culture.

Step Six: Implement your improvements. The benchmarking process should drive the organization to change. There is no point in benchmarking if the leadership is not willing to make changes. Some organizations will go through the motions of studying best-in-class performers without realizing that the objective is to determine what changes need to be made. The benchmarking team needs to develop action plans for implementing change and should then follow through in a systematic manner. Some people will have a vested interest in maintaining the status quo. Please consider the perspectives offered in Chapter 5 regarding methods for developing consensus in academic communities.

Step Seven: Recalibrate the institution. It is not enough to simply implement changes in processes, although this is fundamental to success. The institution must also measure the results after the implementation of the new strategy. Collecting data to measure the results is important to determine if the changes were effective and to reinforce the concept of continuous improvement.

Susan Engelkemeyer, at Babson College, has identified both challenges and benefits of benchmarking for higher educational institutions. Engelkemeyer has studied the results of benchmarking studies conducted by the American Association for Higher Education's (AAHE) Academic Quality Consortium, which was launched by AAHE in 1992.[4] Engelkemeyer has found that benchmarking can be a challenge due to the difficulty in establishing "bottom-line" measures in higher education and difficulties in linking changes in processes to such measures. On the other hand, Engelkemeyer has found that benchmarking stimulates reflective thinking with the campus community, compelling people to critique their processes and to look outside of their institutional traditions for new approaches to better serve their stakeholders.

SUMMARY

The role of institutional leaders in higher education is to constantly monitor the process of internal institutional analysis while keeping track of a dynamic educational environment. Those who focus on maintaining their current processes will fall behind those who are focused on continuous improvement. Once an organization falls behind, it becomes harder and harder to catch up.

Benchmarking provides academic leaders with a structured approach for seeking, identifying, studying, and implementing effective practices that have been developed in other departments, at other campuses, and even in higher educational settings in other nations.

NOTES

1. Xerox Quality Services, *A World of Quality* (Rochester, NY: XQS Press, 1993).

2. Robert C. Camp, *Benchmarking: The Search for Industry Best Practices that Lead to Superior Performance* (Milwaukee, WI: ASQ Quality Press, 1989).

3. University of California Berkeley, *Report of the Chancellor's Exploratory Committee on Continuous Improvement*, Berkeley, CA, 1999.

4. Susan Engelkemeyer, "Applying Benchmarking in Higher Education." *Quality Management Journal* 5, Issue 4, 1998.

CHAPTER 7

Leadership, Consensus, and Teamwork in the Higher Education Community

A healthy academic department is a businesslike social enterprise with a strong sense of its place in the larger college or university enterprise.

—Allan Tucker

Universities present a conundrum when it comes to collaboration, consensus, and working as a team. Few organizational settings espouse collegiality and collaboration more than the academic institution, yet few seem to struggle so much in actually working as a team. While they may attend periodic faculty meetings, faculty members may rarely collaborate with their colleagues in their own department. Faculty members sometimes have more contact with peers at other institutions than with their colleagues in the next office. Others may work more closely with their students than with their peers. Rivalries can be fierce and there can be strong competition over limited resources, teaching loads, graduate assistants, and grants.

Most universities have an extensive number of standing committees, departmental meetings, and staff meetings, yet when it comes to meetings, universities often put the fun in dysfunctional. Committees often exist to preserve the status quo, so their meetings focus on rejecting new ideas and change.

On the other hand, universities that have adopted a philosophy of continuous improvement have shown some great examples of rapidly establishing new academic programs, improving the effectiveness and efficiency of faculty and staff meetings, and creating cross-campus initiatives that improve services to students. Continuous improvement and team building go hand in hand in the academic environment.

In this chapter, leadership, collaboration, and team building in the academy will be examined from the perspective of decision-making styles, tools for building consensus, methods to communicate effectively, understanding the dynamics of meetings, an awareness of the phase theory of groups, the use of 360 degree feedback instruments and through the creation of opportunities for reflective practice among faculty and staff.

CONTINUOUS IMPROVEMENT AND LEADERSHIP

Regardless of whether the organizational context is higher education, health care, government, research, or manufacturing, every continuous improvement initiative immediately touches upon issues of leadership. The continuous improvement body of knowledge blends a great deal of research and application conducted by members of the academic community in the field of organization development with the observations of gurus in the quality movement, such as W. Edwards Deming, and the analysis of leadership in the Malcolm Baldrige National Quality Award.

Deming is recognized as one of the key Westerners to influence the rebuilding of the Japanese economy after the Second World War through the use of principles of quality and continuous improvement. Deming's work is based on his understanding of the profound influence of statistical variation in all processes. His message for American managers was all about leadership. Deming believed that most American companies were poorly led because managers did not understand the fourteen obligations, based on statistical principles, that are incumbent on all managers. These are:

1. Create constancy of purpose toward improvement of products and services with a plan to become competitive and stay in business.
2. Adopt the new philosophy. We are in a new economic age. We can no longer live with commonly accepted levels of delays, mistakes, defective materials, and defective workmanship.
3. Cease dependence on mass inspection.
4. End the practice of awarding business on price tag. Instead, depend on meaningful measures of quality along with price.

5. Find problems. It is management's job to work continually on the system.

6. Institute modern methods of training on the job.

7. Institute modern methods of supervision.

8. Drive out fear so that everyone may work effectively for the company.

9. Break down barriers between departments.

10. Eliminate numerical goals, posters, and slogans for the workforce.

11. Eliminate work standards that prescribe numerical quotas.

12. Remove barriers that stand between the hourly worker and his right to pride of workmanship.

13. Institute a vigorous program of education and retraining.

14. Create a structure in top management that will push every day on the above thirteen points.[1]

Deming's point number 8 is an important one for higher education. The higher education system does generate fear in the processes for tenure and promotion. The implications of Deming's observations about process variation for higher education will be considered in Chapter 9.

LEADERSHIP IN THE BALANCE

Leadership in any higher education setting is a balancing act. Department chairs, deans, directors, provosts, presidents, and chancellors are all constantly engaged in balancing conflicting needs and perspectives.

With this in mind, the challenge for leaders is to balance the need for creating and sustaining consensus within the faculty and staff with the leader's obligation to raise the bar in terms of performance. The continuous improvement tools are particularly effective in helping to achieve this balance. By encouraging benchmarking, the use of balanced score cards (Chapter 9), the analysis of comparative data, the use of strategic planning processes, and the use of national standards, such as the Malcolm Baldrige National Quality Award, leaders can build strong consensus around efforts to raise the bar in performance.

Leaders in higher education must balance the need to empower faculty and staff and the need to stay within boundaries established by charters, trustees, and other forms of state, federal, or denominational rules and regulations. In order to provide this balance, it is vital to develop effective committees, teams, task forces, and an understanding of measurement systems that is grounded in the continuous improvement philosophy, hence the need for Chapters 7, 8, and 9 in this book.

Leaders must balance the needs of different stakeholders in the institution, including parents, students, faculty, staff, alumni, local government, local businesses that provide services to the campus, companies that hire graduates, federal agencies that fund research, and state or denominational bodies that own the campus. Continuous improvement, with its emphasis on listening to stakeholders through focus groups and surveys, the use of 360 degree feedback tools, and its encouragement for establishing common ground in strategic planning and consensus-based decision making, is the ideal philosophical framework and methodology for establishing and maintaining a balance among diverse stakeholder needs and expectations.

The University of Wisconsin–Stout, winner of the Malcolm Baldrige National Quality Award, has developed a very progressive structure for providing balance among stakeholder groups for addressing key strategic and operational indicators on its campus. Chancellor Charles W. Sorensen has implemented a Chancellor's Advisory Council, with twenty members that include senior leadership, governance groups, and internal stakeholders. This council establishes organizational direction, ensures broad communication within the campus community, and enables stakeholders to participate in the discussion of issues and priorities.[2]

Joseph Juran observed that people in the private sector speak different languages. Senior managers primarily speak the language of money. Factory workers speak a language of things—machines, tools, products. Middle managers, Juran noted, must be adept at translating the language of money into the language of things, and vice versa, for organizations to succeed.[3]

Higher Education is more complex than the private sector in terms of the languages one must master in order to effectively lead. There is the general language of the academic community, complete with nuances for each academic discipline, as well as the language of money used in budgeting, advancement, and planning. There are also special languages related to athletics, donors, and the ability to understand the encoded phrases of politicians.

LEADERSHIP AND ETHICS

The Malcolm Baldrige National Quality Award presents higher education with an interesting challenge in the need to develop a framework for defining and discussing ethical issues in the higher education context. Although there is a great deal of discussion and training about ethics in business and in health care, the topic has not been well explored in higher education. This is one example of how a higher educational institution benefits by comparing itself against a yardstick like the Baldrige criteria.

While there may be written expectations regarding students' honesty on exams, as well as ethos that abhors plagiarism and state regulations to control the expenditures of state funds, the ethical territory beyond these familiar topics is often rather murky and in need of discussion and clarification on some campuses.

The recognition of a lack of scope and definition of ethics resulting from a comparison of the university to the Baldrige criteria, for example, has led The University of Alabama to establish a small team of distinguished faculty, human resources staff, and legal staff to explore and further define issues of potential ethical concern.

LEADERSHIP AND DECISION-MAKING STYLES

One of the greatest sources of conflict within the academy may be the lack of articulation and agreement on the appropriate style of decision making for a faculty or staff group. In this case, there is nothing as practical as a bit of theory to help create a model and language that enables faculty and staff to discuss how they want to make decisions.

Kurt Lewin proposed an early model to describe leadership styles and decision making.[4] At the same time, Bradford and Lippitt offered a similar model of leadership and decision making, which was further refined by Tannenbaum and Schmitt in the 1950s.[5]

Figure 7.1 is a model of leadership behaviors in the academic setting, based on the work of Lewin, Bradford and Lippitt, and Tannenbaum and Schmitt. This model illustrates the manner in which a dean, chair, or director may make a decision and the impact of the decision-making style on the involvement and commitment of the faculty and staff.

On the left side of the model, the leader makes all the important decisions and announces them to the faculty and staff. This has been referred to as the "hard-boiled autocratic" approach to decision making. In this case, the leader often believes that he or she has more knowledge or expertise than the rest of the faculty or staff, or perceives that the group cannot be entrusted with making decisions due to poor performance. In some cases, this type of leader has only been exposed to this style of decision making and is not aware that other models may exist. The scale on the right side of Figure 7.1 indicates that the faculty and staff involvement in these decisions is low, therefore their commitment to implementing them is also low. In situations of this type, the faculty and staff are resentful and will either leave, become sullen, or adopt a compliant

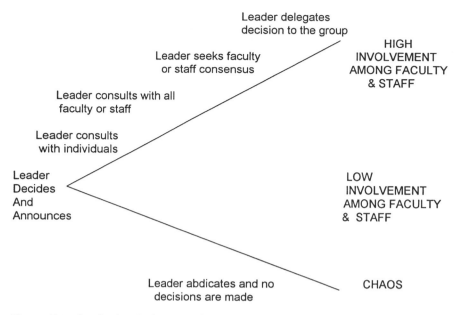

Figure 7.1   Leadership Styles in Higher Education

attitude. The leader's decisions may be ignored by the group when they do not feel they will be punished.

Moving higher along the upper line of the model, we come to the leader who consults with individual faculty or staff members. The leader seeks input from faculty and staff members, but they do not know what other faculty and staff members have said. Based on partial input, or even input from every member of the department, the leader then makes a decision and announces it. Faculty or staff members may recognize their input as having influenced the decision, or they may find their input was disturbingly ignored. Without knowing what input others provided, people may not understand how a particular decision was reached. Leaders may consciously or unconsciously slip into a pattern of consulting with only a few of the faculty or staff. Those who are left out will feel threatened.

The next position along the upper line describes the leader who consults with the faculty and/or staff members in a meeting. Everyone expresses his or her view, and then the leader makes the final decision. In this case, everyone's voice is heard and everyone knows what advice was given or what position was taken by the others in the group. The leader may feel that he or she must retain the final authority for making the decision.

The next level on the upper line represents leaders who allow the decisions to be a consensus of the group. (*Consensus* will be defined later in the chapter.) In this case, the leader encourages discussion and brings the group toward agreeing upon an outcome that everyone can support. It may take longer to achieve consensus. And because faculty often values debate, often looking for differences rather than consensus, it may be difficult to achieve. However, decisions that are reached by consensus have higher involvement by the faculty and/or staff members, who are more likely to support and implement the decision.

The highest level on this scale is the leader who delegates the authority to the faculty or staff to make a decision, within some defined boundaries. The boundaries may be related to budgets, deadlines, conditions of a grant or gift, or state or institutional policies. In this instance, the leader delegates authority to the group and does not participate in the discussion. Many search committees are expected to operate in this fashion. A president, or provost, delegates the search to a committee, and if the committee stays within the proper boundaries, it should bring forth an acceptable candidate.

This model is very beneficial for discussion within faculty and staff meetings to give people a common understanding, a visual model, and a language to describe what happens within their work group. The lack of this common frame of reference can be the source of bitter conflict within departments and colleges. An administrator may believe it is perfectly good, right, and normal to gather individual input and make a decision and announce it. A faculty or staff member may strongly believe that the decision should be made in a group meeting, perhaps by consensus. Without a model that can be used to frame the nature of the conflict, a working relationship can be destroyed when the two parties disagree over the process by which a decision is made. With a model, it is much easier for administrators, faculty, and staff to describe the nature of their conflict and to reach a common understanding.

Another common problem is the new department chair, dean, or director who prefers to make autocratic decisions and takes over a group that has been accustomed to consensus-based decision making. The faculty or staff will be in shock as decisions are made and announced without their voices being heard.

In looking at this model, faculty and staff members often believe they want to stay permanently in the upper right hand corner, with all decisions made by consensus or even delegated to them. However, faculty or staff groups that rely heavily on consensus frequently complain that they have to spend too much time making trivial decisions. The ultimate application of this model is for faculty and staff to use it to enter into a discussion and consensus regarding which decisions they think should be made autocratically by their dean, chair, and/or director and which should be made through consensus. When this consensus can be reached, the source of many conflicts is removed. For example, Binghamton University's Psychology Department's "Structure and Function Team" established boundaries on which decisions were to be made through consensus and which were in the purview of the department's executive committee. This clarity has worked very well for the department.

The model also recognizes that some leaders fail to lead. Lewin referred to this as laissez-faire leadership, or the absence of leadership. It means simply letting the group do whatever it wants to do. Problems are not addressed, there is no strategic plan for the organization, staff meetings are infrequent and unfocused. This may be the result of professional burnout or preoccupation with more enjoyable activities, such as conducting research, leading a professional society, or writing. Having a model helps people name the problem when it happens.

In a world that is becoming more international and where change has become the rule rather than the exception, many view the role of the leader as having also changed. The new leader is viewed as one who is a mentor, coach, a facilitator, and a visionary. The new leader must empower those who work for him or her and create an atmosphere of interdependency. The new leader must also create an atmosphere in which staff members have the ability and are encouraged to disagree. Finally, the new leader must focus on the future, for with change coming so fast, the organization must have a clear purpose and a clear sense of where it is going.

BUILDING CONSENSUS

Consensus is not the same thing as majority rule. In majority rule, there is a majority that "wins" and usually a minority that "loses." Voting can be a clear and quick way to reach a decision, but it sometimes leaves people with the feeling that they have been defeated, and they may not be supportive in implementing the decision that has been reached.

Political democracy in municipal, state, and federal government relies on voting and majority rule, but organizational democracy relies on developing a consensus in which people will consent to work together.

Consensus decision making has the following characteristics that are different from majority rule and from autocratic decision making:

1. There is an emphasis on dialogue and on understanding other people's points of view.
2. People are encouraged to generate many options and even invent new options as they go along.
3. The objective is a win-win outcome, not win-lose.
4. Everyone can "buy-in" at least 70 percent with the decision that is made.
5. No one ends up with serious heartburn over the decision.

Reaching a consensus about which issues require the faculty and/or staff's participation and which issues are delegated to the chair or director is a fundamental issue. The sooner this agreement can be clarified and established, the sooner a department will function effectively. This consensus about decision making can certainly be renegotiated over time as the team matures. Without agreement about how decisions will be made, trust will erode.

Binghamton builds consensus in meetings by establishing agreement on the ground rules for conducting a meeting and the use of the LUIS model. Binghamton uses the following rules to help make team meetings more efficient, productive, and to foster an atmosphere conducive to collegiality and teamwork. Team members can add additional rules they would like to use to guide their meetings, and the entire team should reach a consensus that it will follow these rules at all of its meetings.

1. Begin on time;
2. End on time;
3. Everyone at the meeting is equal;
4. Attend all meetings;
5. Listen to and show respect for the views of other members;
6. No side conversations or side looks;
7. Don't give solutions but rather find causes first;
8. Focus on or criticize problems or symptoms and not the person;
9. Carry out assignments on time;
10. No meetings outside the meeting;
11. Share information, not attitudes.

The LUIS model helps people understand the meaning of consensus.

PHASE ONE
EXPLORING

PHASE TWO
FOCUSING

PHASE THREE
CLOSURE

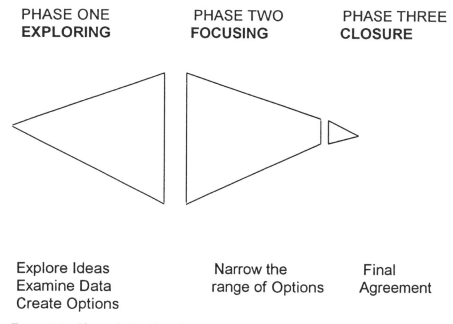

Explore Ideas
Examine Data
Create Options

Narrow the
range of Options

Final
Agreement

Figure 7.2   Phases for Building Consensus

L   I can live with this decision.
U   I understand this decision.
I   I was involved in this decision.
S   I will support this decision.

Figure 7.2 illustrates the nature of consensus building in a group. In the first phase, the group needs time to explore ideas, examine data, and create options. In the second phase, the group needs to begin to narrow down the ideas it will consider and focus on the best options. In the third phase, the group needs to reach a consensus regarding which idea or decision is the best.

The exploring phase may engage faculty and/or staff in reviewing data or in creating ideas and options. To stimulate the generation of ideas, the group may use a brainstorming exercise. However, brainstorming sometimes falls flat within a team when the dynamics are poor for creative thinking. This occurs when people are not having fun, when they have been sitting still for a long time, and when their energy level is low. Because many people think best when they are moving and able to draw fully on their senses, exercise and movement help brainstorming.

Experts in creative thinking have noted that having fun is fundamental to the creative process.[6] Providing team members with kinesthetic aids is both fun and a sound method based on the established patterns and preferences that many people have for processing information. Examples of good kinesthetic aids to stimulate brainstorming in teams are yo-yos, play-dough, building blocks, and any type of small, squeezable ball that people can hold in their hands and toss at one another without hurting anyone. Make these toys available and stand back as faculty and staff members grab an object that gives them pleasure by connecting them with positive memories and experiences.

The focusing phase requires the group to begin to narrow the range of options and ideas they will pursue. Nominal Group Technique (NGT) is a quick way to help a group explore and then prioritize their options.[7] There are several variations of nominal group technique. The following are basic steps:

1. Start by being clear about what the issue is that requires a decision.
2. List the options on an easel where everyone can see them.
3. Give team members a few minutes to discuss the options and let people voice their opinions as to the pros and cons of the options.
4. Give each person a set of colored dots to place by each of the ideas they consider to be the best. (The number of dots each person gets depends on the number of options from which they must chose. The general rule of thumb is to divide the number of options by three to determine the number of dots. Thirty options means ten dots for each participant.) In other cases, participants can be asked to numerically rank their choices, with the first choice receiving the highest number.
5. The visual distribution of the dots shows where the consensus of the group may be.

The closure phase means stating clearly what the consensus of the group appears to be, checking with all group members to ensure there is no serious heartburn, and then moving on to deciding how to implement the choice, or as stated in the LUIS model: I can live with this decision, I understand this decision, I was involved in this decision, and I will support this decision.

An additional challenge to reaching consensus among faculty is the need for consensus about process before attempting to reach consensus on content. It is important for faculty to feel that the process being used for making a decision is fair and will result in legitimate outcomes. Only when there is consensus about process can there be an opportunity to develop consensus about content.

FOCUS OF MEETINGS

Within the faculty, and within the administration, there is a need for frequent meetings to plan, make decisions, share information, and solve problems. Some meetings are effective and some are not, so it is important to develop effective meeting habits.

Faculty and staff members should first recognize that they have a sphere of influence and a sphere of concern. Usually, the sphere of concern is greater than their sphere of influence. Spending time on issues that are outside of the faculty or staff's sphere of influence is usually not productive.[8]

The sphere of influence includes all the things the faculty or staff can actually do something about. This includes decisions about allocation of faculty and staff time and resources, decisions related to academic programs and standards, and their own attitudes about participation and collegiality. Meetings that focus on what the faculty (or staff) control will have positive results.

The sphere of concerns includes all the things that the faculty or staff may be concerned about, such as pay, support for conferences, increasing faculty numbers, attracting good students, and getting published. Some of these concerns will fall within the faculty and staff's sphere of influence. In these cases, the faculty and staff members may be able to effectively address their concerns if they are able to work together effectively. In other cases, the concerns are outside of the sphere of influence of the faculty or staff. In these situations, the faculty and staff have only two choices. One is to not spend any time on the concern, since it is outside the sphere of influence, and the other choice is to work to expand the faculty (or staff) sphere of influence to be able to address these issues of concern.

In working with teams and offices, a good way to explain the sphere of concerns and sphere of influence is to advise teams or offices that they should not try to tackle or solve issues where the power for implementing the solution is more than one level above them. For example, if an office wants to change a process but the rules that govern the process are determined by an agency outside the campus (e.g., the governor's office), then that would not be a good process to undertake to change. If a director or dean empowers a team, but the power to implement the solution rests at a level above the vice president, this would also not be a good project to initially undertake. Teams need success in their initial attempt to work together. By using this guideline, facilitators have a much better chance of achieving success in implementing the solutions that a team arrives at through consensus.

There are all sorts of issues that faculty or staff might select to work on during meetings. Some issues are urgent, others are not. Some issues are important, while others are not. Faculty and staff can use nominal group technique to rank order the issues from the most to least urgent and then address issues one at a time. After rank ordering the issues, a group can be asked to evaluate the top issues to ensure that they are doable in a short period of time, since it is important to achieve early successes as a group learns to function as a team. Sometimes a team may choose to begin on issues that they ranked 3, 4, 5, and 7 because they are more easily solved. Then, after learning the process of working as a team, they can take on the difficult issues. It helps teams to take "baby steps" first to ensure success. It can be helpful to construct a meetings matrix that helps faculty and staff groups keep track of the issues they are working on. Figure 7.3 illustrates the nature of urgency and importance in a meeting, and segments these into four quadrants, which are derived from Covey's model of time management.

Issues in quadrant one are both important and urgent. These may be crisis decisions or problems that need to be solved, such as who will fill in for a faculty member who has become ill. Quadrant one issues must be resolved in a timely manner for the school or college to be successful. However, no organization really wants to continuously have meetings devoted to quadrant one issues.

	URGENT	NOT URGENT
IMPORTANT	1 *Crisis Decisions*	2 *Planning Self-Assessments Continuous Improvement*
NOT IMPORTANT	3 *Information Sharing*	4 *Self-Centered Behaviors*

Figure 7.3   Use of Time in Faculty and Staff Meetings

Issues in quadrant two are important, but not urgent. This is the quadrant that includes activities such as conducting self-assessments, planning of the coming semester and year, identification of potential problems, and discussion about how a course or process can be improved. Effective use of quadrant two helps keep an organization from spending a lot of time in quadrant one.

Quadrant three describes the issues that are not really important but are urgent and require brief action. These are often information-sharing activities, such as reminding everyone when grades are due or when bookstore orders must be placed. These issues need to be addressed but should be addressed quickly.

The issues in quadrant four are neither urgent nor important. These are the times when people tell personal stories, complain about issues outside their sphere of influence, brag about their research or their golf game. This quadrant does not add value to achieving the organization's mission or vision but are self-centered behaviors. When people realize their meeting has drifted into quadrant four, they need to get back into a more productive quadrant.

To be effective, faculty and staff need to maximize the time spent working in quadrant two on things that are important but not yet urgent. Maximizing the work in quadrant two enables faculty and staff groups to stay out of quadrant one (fire fighting) by keeping the fires from starting in the first place.

USING A PARKING LOT

Sometimes people come up with ideas in a meeting that will derail the progress being made by dragging everyone off onto some tangent. Some issues arise that are too volatile to be addressed immediately in a faculty or staff meeting. For both these reasons, it is effective for the faculty (or staff) to maintain a "parking lot" where issues can be parked for future discussion. When an issue comes up that needs to be addressed, but not immediately, the faculty can agree to put the issue in the parking lot to be saved for future discussion. This allows a meeting to stay focused on the most important issues that people came prepared to discuss without losing track of other issues that need to be handled. Issues in the parking lot can be addressed at the close of the meeting, if there is time, or can be put on the agenda for a future meeting. When using a parking lot, it is vital to honor the principle and to bring the items out for discussion in a timely manner. Otherwise, people will consider it a garbage can where their idea or concern is being dumped instead of being saved for future discussion.

PHASE THEORY OF GROUPS

The members of a faculty group, a staff organization, or the leadership team of a college or university are subject to constant change over time. It is useful to be aware of the theory of phase movement that describes how groups transition through a variety of predictable phases over the life of the group. There are at least a dozen approaches to identifying and classifying the phase movement of groups.[9]

For the purpose of reflecting on groups in academe, a five-phase model can be used to describe groups in a start-up phase, a testing phase, a performance phase, a retesting phase, and a close-out phase. Department chairs, deans, directors, provosts, and presidents can use health charts to evaluate the well-being of their groups in each of these phases.

The start-up phase describes the dynamics when a new program has been launched, when there is a high amount of staff or faculty turnover, or when some type of interdisciplinary team is formed to address an issue. In the start-up phase, it is important to clarify the group's mission, develop agreement on how decisions are going to be made, understand the group's limits or boundaries, establish a mechanism for communicating and conducting meetings, and ensure that all stakeholders who need to be included are represented in an appropriate manner.

In the testing phase, the group may fall apart by not meeting or by not reaching early consensus on how to proceed. In this phase, people are testing each other to see if they can work together, and they are testing their boundaries to see what they are really going to be allowed to do. Special attention needs to be focused on early signs of dysfunctional behavior, such as people not attending meetings, excessive use of meeting time for quadrant four issues, or refusal to discuss important issues.

When groups mature into the performance phase, there are issues to monitor to ensure continued healthy performance. It is vital to make sure that the group does continue to meet on some regular basis. In the performance phase, the group may see its sphere of influence expand due to successes.

Academic leaders should remain alert to recognize when a group has moved from the performance phase into the retesting phase. In this case, membership in the group may have changed or conditions in which the group operates, such as budget, may have changed. Does the group need to be recharged through a retreat? Does it need to conduct a self-assessment and develop new plans? Have group members hurt each other's feelings over the course of time? All of these are normal parts of the life cycle of a group and should be anticipated.

In some cases, it is appropriate to bring a group to closure, or the close-out phase. Departments may need to be merged or eliminated. Committees may outlive their usefulness. Interdisciplinary research projects come to an end. If closure is needed, it is important to plan an event that provides a sense of finality and recognition for contributions that have been made during the life of the group.

HUMAN RESOURCES ISSUES

Like corporations and government agencies, universities have attempted to implement modern practices of human resource (HR) management. Unfortunately, HR professionals have introduced some counterproductive activities that have been widely criticized among continuous improvement leaders. The most notable problem that HR has inflicted on higher education is importation of performance review processes that do not work in the corporate world. Dr. Deming has noted that, at best, performance appraisals add no value and, at worst, they harm employees and make them angry. Deming applied a statistician's critique to human performance and noted that in most organizations, 95 percent of the employees are doing the best job that their work system will possibly allow them to do. Perhaps as many as 5 percent are not well suited for their job or have performance problems and need coaching. Subjecting everyone to a review process in order to address the problem of 5 percent makes little sense. Attempts to link performance to pay are futile, since most people's performance is linked to the overall effectiveness of the system.

Western Wisconsin Technical College has studied Deming's observations and has improved its Human Resources program by eliminating blanket performance reviews for all employees.[10] WWTC relies on the traditional probationary period to identify and weed out employees with early performance problems. All employees develop an Employee Success Plan that describes what they will do in the future to continually improve their performance and to grow as professionals.

360 DEGREE FEEDBACK INSTRUMENTS

Academic institutions often have very structured and legalistic methods for evaluating performance. Department chairs and deans are usually subject to a review by their faculty on a periodic basis. Faculty are subject to annual reviews by their department chairs. Promotional decisions are made in highly structured peer review processes.

Opportunities for improvement are often missed during performance reviews. People are more concerned about keeping their jobs or obtaining a promotion than they are about listening for ideas for continued growth and improvement. Administrators are often known to step down from a position rather than open themselves up for criticism in performance reviews from faculty. Others, who fear being held accountable in annual reviews by their director or vice president, go through an elaborate sham each year of establishing performance goals that they cannot possibly miss, so they will not be graded down during their evaluations. Performance reviews and peer reviews often do not contribute to continuous improvement in the academic setting.

Some schools have experimented with "360 degree" feedback instruments that are separate from the performance review process. These instruments allow administrators to receive feedback from the people they lead, their peers, and their dean or director, in a nonthreatening way. The participants select a group of people who will complete feedback forms. The information from the forms is collated by a third party so that the recipient will not know exactly which person provided which feedback. The individual can then compare feedback on a structure set of questions from a diverse set of people with whom he or she works everyday.

Appendix 1 is a copy of the 360 Degree Feedback Instrument used at The University of Alabama.

REFLECTIVE PRACTICE

There are many ways to improve the performance of an academic or administrative group. One way is to invest some time to talk about how the group is working. This discussion can help faculty and/or staff members assess where they are in the life cycle of the group, and it can make it possible for group members to talk about their performance strengths and weaknesses in a positive way.

One effective method for helping a group learn more about itself is through the use of a metaphor for discussion. This is often done effectively by identifying one or more metaphors that helps people discuss their group's performance in a nonthreatening way. This is one approach of a methodology known as "reflective practice."

Reflective practice is a concept pioneered among adult educators to create new learning about life situations. As a learning tool, reflective practice involves people in critiquing the presuppositions on which their beliefs about a situation have been built.[11] Educators employ a variety of tools to stimulate reflective thinking, such as group discussion, structured interviewing techniques, role playing, and workshops. Reflective practice sessions enable people to critique their participation in a group and to challenge one another's thinking in order to gain self-insight.[12]

A reflective practice session in the academic setting brings participants together and starts by using exercises and ideas that help people "get out of the box" to create new understandings about how the group functions on a daily basis.

Binghamton University uses the Metaphor Game to encourage new understandings about how an organization functions and what it feels like to be part of that organization.[13] Participants are asked to describe their organization as a voyage, as a game, as a war, as a machine, and as an organism. In each case, people engage in fresh discussion about their organization and may share some new insights about the strengths and weaknesses of the organization. Participants can then be asked to identify specific actions that could be taken to improve the organization's weaknesses.

In some cases, it works well to use a sports metaphor to open up dialogue within an academic setting. Many groups can correspond their work to a particular sporting event, and many (but not all) people are sports enthusiasts and will relate to a sports metaphor once they understand how it connects to their work. The use of a sports metaphor is another way to encourage creative thinking in the organization as people use the metaphor to redefine their working relationships. Using this kind of open dialogue allows some tough truths to surface in a healthy manner.

There are obvious similarities between work and sports. Both activities involve rules and boundaries that must be observed. Team sports, like work, require an understanding of who will do what and when. Team sports and the academic workplace both have a roster of "players" who exercise certain skills as well as "others" who have a stake in the outcome. The sport team's performance is recorded and analyzed for improvement opportunities, just as the performance of an academic or administrative group can be documented and analyzed for continuous improvement.

To prepare for a reflective practice session using a sports metaphor, the event planner must first determine what sports metaphor really fits his or her organization. Many faculty groups are like track and field teams, where individuals perform (teach, research, publish) and are evaluated individually, but the overall group's performance is assessed based on the combined output of the group. Staff organizations, on the other hand, tend to correlate with the basketball metaphor, where the ball is often moved around to set up a successful play.

To facilitate this type of reflective practice, a time and location need to be identified when all group members can participate without feeling rushed. In most cases, it is wise to conduct the session in a location away from the faculty or staff offices.

Having decided on which sports metaphor to use, a list of discussion questions should be prepared. These questions are intended to capture the participant's imaginations in order to catch him or her up in the metaphor. The person who will lead the session should fully explore the selected sports metaphor to capitalize on facilitating discussion points. The discussion questions should not be given to the participants prior to the session. Special arrangements can be made to foster a sense of teamwork. A small token, such as a pencil with the appropriate sports teams, can be provided to participants to represent the theme of the meeting.

To conduct this type of reflective practice session, the leader will first ask the participants to define the similarities between their organization and the sport. Ask the participants to identify similarities; they should be asked to identify what role or position they each play. Next, ask the group to consider how the rules of this sport would fit their organization. What are examples of unsportsmanlike conduct, for example, in their context? Build on the metaphor as much as possible and encourage people to have fun with it.

After the metaphor has been fully explored, introduce the idea of reviewing the game film. This is what sports teams do to continuously improve. Ask the group to identify examples of excellence they have experienced while they have been in this organization. Take one or two examples and ask the participants to explain exactly what they did that made them successful. Identify these as the organization's success factors.

Then, ask the participants to examine an example where they were not successful. Ask them to look at their list of success factors and identify which items they did not do well that resulted in the poor performance. This is powerful learning.

The Registrar's Office at The University of Alabama has used the sports metaphor effectively. They selected gymnastics as their sport and quickly identified similarities between the three concurrent events at a gym meet and the three concurrent tasks of their organization. They had fun discussing their organizational equivalents of the gym meet. In reviewing their game film, they looked at a successful project and clearly identified the things they had done that made them successful. In reviewing a less than stellar project, they quickly recognized which of their success factors they had not effectively addressed.

There are many reasons to use a reflective practice session to develop teamwork within an academic or administrative unit. First, people in organizations often become complacent about issues in their culture that are unhealthy or dysfunctional. People may have become lax about reporting problems or may be reluctant to offer suggestions for improvement. There may be systemic problems with the manner in which people communicate or confusion over the roles that people are expected to play. The reflective practice exercises that employ sports as a metaphor give people a safe opportunity to surface the issues that need to be discussed.

Reflective practice creates a sudden, and often unexpected, opportunity for people to express their feelings about issues that often go unaddressed. Instead of denying that problems exist, concerns are safely brought to the surface and can be addressed within the established framework of the sports metaphor. Reviewing the game film requires everyone to acknowledge both the strengths and the weaknesses of the team and offers an opportunity for people to pull together.

LEADERSHIP DEVELOPMENT

Community colleges, colleges, and universities are all greatly dependent on the quality of their leadership in developing and executing effective plans and in providing the appropriate balance of stakeholder perspectives and collaboration to enable an institution to accomplish its goals. With so much riding on leadership, many institutions are focusing resources on leadership development as a component of their continuous improvement efforts.

Pennsylvania State University initiated an Excellence in Leadership and Management Program in 1998. This is a comprehensive program that provides professional development for leaders at all levels of the Penn State campus. It Includes the Penn State Leader program, Mastering SuperVision, a Management Institute, and a Leadership Academy for new department chairs and division directors.

Cornell University has initiated a Discovering Leadership Program that offers a series of developmental activities that help participants discover their leadership strengths and areas for growth. The program promotes self-understanding and the development of technical abilities necessary for achieving effective teamwork and for leading change in the campus environment. Participants are engaged in eleven days of workshops over a five-month period.[14]

The University of Alabama has instituted a Leadership Academy for faculty and academic and nonacademic administrators. Participants attend ten days of workshops and seminars over a two-year period. An orientation program has also been developed for new academic department chairs, along with a management program for all new and prospective supervisors in nonacademic units.

SUMMARY

Continuous improvement efforts stimulate the development of consensus and teamwork on a campus by encouraging dialogue regarding strategic planning and self-assessments, collaboration to improve processes, and communication with stakeholder groups. Although there is much discussion about collegiality in the academic setting, many faculty and staff members become entrenched in disputes and competition for resources that undermine the spirit of collaboration. With its emphasis on engaging faculty and staff in planning, assessment, and improvement, the continuous improvement methodology turns out to be an effective way to build consensus and to encourage teamwork.

NOTES

1. W. Edwards Deming, *Quality, Productivity, and Competitive Position* (Cambridge, MA: Massachusetts Institute of Technology, 1982).

2. Charles W. Sorensen and Diane Moen, "Winning the Baldrige National Quality Award," in *Pursuing Excellence in Higher Education* (San Francisco: Jossey-Bass, 2004).

3. Joseph Juran, *Managerial Breakthrough* (New York: McGraw-Hill, 1964).

4. Kurt Lewin, "The Practicality of Democracy," *Human Nature and Enduring Peace* (Boston: Houghton Mifflin, 1945).

5. Leland P. Bradford, and Ronald Lippitt, "Building a Democratic Work Group," *Personnel* 22 (1945): 3.

6. Doug Hall, *Jump Start Your Brain* (New York: Warner Books, 1995).

7. Donald C. Mosley, "Nominal Grouping as an Organizational Development Intervention Technique," *Training and Development Journal* (March 1974): 30–37.

8. Stephen R. Covey, *The 7 Habits of Highly Effective People* (New York: Simon & Shuster, 1989).

9. Malcolm Knowles and Hulda Knowles, *Introduction to Group Dynamics* (New York: Follett Publishing, 1972).

10. Lee Rasch, "Quality . . . The Western Way," NCCI Conference, 2002.

11. Jack Mezirow, *Fostering Critical Reflection in Adulthood* (San Francisco: Jossey-Bass, 1990).

12. Victoria J. Marsick, "Action Learning and Reflection in the Workplace," in *Fostering Critical Reflection in Adulthood*, ed. Jack Mezirow (San Francisco: Jossey-Bass, 1990).

13. Billie S. Willits and Leonard E. Pollack, "Penn State's Excellence in Leadership and Management Program," in *Pursuing Excellence in Higher Education* (San Franscisco: Jossey-Bass, 2004).

14. Chester C. Warzynski, "Leadership Development at Cornell University," in *Pursuing Excellence in Higher Education* (San Francisco: Jossey-Bass, 2004).

CHAPTER

Facilitating Campus Teams

The focus on continuous improvement of every process to meeting internal as well as external customer needs requires us to change the way we think of organizational structure.
—John Harris, Samford University

In the 1960s, Joseph Juran noted that continuous improvement in many organizational settings required cooperation across traditional organizational boundaries.[1] The push for continuous improvement in organizations has accelerated the use of teams at all levels in business, government, health care, and education, spurred on by a high level of academic research in group dynamics and team effectiveness theory. Early academic research in team behaviors in the 1940s and 1950s was incorporated into the continuous improvement body of knowledge in the 1980s by organizations such as the Association for Quality and Productivity, the Quality and Productivity Management Association, and the American Productivity and Quality Center.

Teamwork and continuous improvement are so closely intertwined now that it is difficult to separate the two concepts. What most teams work on are continuous improvement issues, and most improvement activities require a team to make breakthroughs.

This chapter will examine the types of team activities that should occur on campuses that adopt a continuous improvement philosophy and will highlight some practical tools that help build team effectiveness.

Two varieties of teams will be found in most academic and nonacademic organizations. Teams that pull together people from various organizations in order to improve a process or address a campuswide issue are categorized as "cross-functional teams." Teams that are made up wholly of faculty or staff within a department or college are generally referred to as "natural work teams." The dynamics of these two teams are similar in some respects and different in others. Cross-functional teams are generally created in some formal manner and are not intended to last forever, although they can be institutionalized into a standing committee. Natural work teams emerge from within the organization, often because of a director or department chair who has mastered the art of leading people in a highly participative manner.

CROSS-FUNCTIONAL TEAMS

There are many opportunities for quality improvement in the academic environment that require the use of cross-functional teams. The formation of a cross-functional team will require the following:

1. A clear problem, cluster of problems, or strategic issue that requires attention and can be used to focus the team and help define its boundaries. Cross-functional teams need some type of official charge or charter to give them legitimacy.

2. At least one senior person in the organization who will champion the formation of the cross-functional team and provide a senior-level perspective on issues related to the team and who will guide the team through the organization's political paths. This senior person will act as a sponsor for the team and may be the executive who has the money or power to implement the team's recommendations.

3. Team members who represent the views of all the stakeholders who have an interest in the problem(s) and who are empowered to speak and act on behalf of their respective organizations. Team members should be directly involved with the issue they are addressing. A team of five to seven people is an optimal size.

4. A neutral facilitator who is familiar with a wide range of group processes and quality tools and who will guide the team and keep it moving while remaining neutral regarding the content.

5. Meeting space and location conducive to group work.

6. Adequate time for the team members to diagnose the situation, participate in collegial discussion, and to develop plans that fit the culture of the institution. It is often helpful to set a date by which the team will

conclude its work in order to ensure that the diagnosis does not get drawn out over too long a period of time.

Juran observed that cross-functional teams embark on two journeys—a diagnostic journey and a remedial journey.[2] The cross-functional team in higher education will typically be engaged in both these journeys, so Juran's model is useful for this context.

During the diagnostic journey, the team defines the issues it needs to address, sorts these issues out into manageable pieces, and decides on the sequence in which to address these issues. It is important for the team to make it through this first step. If the team cannot agree on what the issues are, or the sequence in which to address the issues, the team will never get out of the gate. In this first step, the team is "framing" the issues it will address.[3] The manner in which issues are defined, or the framework in which they are perceived, is critical and will profoundly impact all further actions.

The team will then move on to address specific parts of an issue, usually by collecting data through a variety of means. Often the team members must educate one another by sharing their perspectives and knowledge about an issue. Additional data may come from a wide variety of sources and can be organized and analyzed with the various tools in the quality tool kit, such as run charts, Pareto diagrams, cause and effect diagrams, control charts, flowcharts, and other methods. Each team will be seeking solutions to problems and ideas for improving the process.

The process of sharing information and learning about a process is not without some potential emotional difficulties for the participants. Some people may feel defensive about the role their organization plays in a process and may have positions they want to defend. Others may harbor feelings of blame and may be interested in venting their frustration rather than making improvements. The facilitator must be ready to deal with these potential problems.

The diagnostic journey is the point where the team needs to be able to draw upon a wide variety of continuous improvement tools and concepts to diagnose the situation. The role of the facilitator is to introduce the most appropriate tools to help in the journey, drawing upon the data collection, statistical tools, and tools for facilitating change that are described in Chapter 3. Facilitators should be knowledgeable about all these tools and know when to apply them. The old adage among facilitators is that if the only tool you have is a hammer, every problem looks like a nail.

The degree to which cross-functional team members participate in the remedial journey varies greatly. The remedial journey is the implementation of the process improvements and changes that result from the diagnostic journey. In some cases, cross-functional team members are only expected to recommend a course of action that may need approval by a council of deans, a provost, vice president, or president. In other cases, the team is expected to implement the ideas for improvement that it creates while keeping the appropriate champion or administrator informed. The boundaries for the cross-functional team regarding the remedial journey should be defined when the team is created.

It is generally advisable to provide the cross-functional team with a written charter that defines the scope of its project, any boundaries it must stay within, and any expectations regarding its role in implementing changes. This charter provides the team members with legitimacy within the campus and gives them the authority they may need to collect data from administrative or academic groups, to conduct surveys, to organize focus groups, or other actions necessary to diagnose a situation.

Binghamton University, for example, created a cross-functional team called the "Orientation Team" to address the need and opportunity to improve the student summer orientation process by focusing on how new students register for courses. The team was created by two champions— the vice provost for Planning and Budget and the assistant vice president for Student Life. Team members were drawn from a variety of organizations that were stakeholders in the orientation process, including faculty, the registrar's office, enrollment management, advising, and campus activities. The champions requested assistance from Binghamton's Center for Quality to provide neutral facilitation for the team.

The orientation team focused on the problem that new students have when requesting courses during July orientation without knowing until late August whether they are actually registered. The team wanted to find a way to use the existing computer registration system in a "real time" mode so students would have a schedule of registered classes in hand when they left orientation. Team members had to share information with each other about the capacities of the existing system and consulted with outside offices to confirm the feasibility and benefits of their proposals. Through their redesign of the process, the team members were able to eliminate the bias toward first-arriving registrants, to handle a large number of students registering on-line at the same time, and to provide students with academic advisors on the spot if selected courses were closed. The team members were responsible for both the diagnostic journey and the remedial journey and implemented their proposals during the summer of 2001.[4]

Over the last ten years, Pennsylvania State University has had hundreds of cross-functional teams working in almost every part of the campus. Over a dozen continuous improvement teams have worked on issues related to alumni in the past ten years. Most projects focus on a specific activity or process that needs to be improved. Alumni Relations, for example, partnered with Undergraduate Programs in the College of Liberal Arts in a cross-functional effort to improve the process for identifying the addresses of international alumni.[5]

In another example, the Graduate School at the University of Wisconsin–Madison formed a cross-functional team with members from admissions, academic student services, fellowships, a transcript examiner, and an admissions coordinator to examine and improve the admissions process for the graduate school. The process was far too cumbersome and slow, causing the graduate school to lose many excellent candidates.

The project team mapped out the flow of the admissions process and collected data over an eighteen-month period to establish the baseline performance of the process. With these data, the team could understand how long it took to process examiners' reports, the time required to receive an admissions recommendation, and the total time for an admissions decision. With the baseline data, the team found it took ninety-nine days, on average, to admit a student, with twenty-six of the days being time that the admissions staff handled the paperwork.

The team examined problems in each step of the process and contacted other universities in a benchmarking exercise to find better methods for performing the same tasks. Through benchmarking, the team found an institution that was turning around admissions decisions in five days.

Based on benchmarking and process analysis, the team redesigned the admissions process. Admission time was reduced by 39 percent. The backlog of admissions work was eliminated, and admissions costs were reduced by 38 percent.[6]

At the University of Miami, a cross-functional team on student housing focused on improving the availability of housing and decreasing the cost of providing student housing. The team's efforts led to an increase in the number of students in campus housing and a 41 percent decrease in overtime hours required to provide the housing.[7]

NATURAL WORK TEAMS

In many cases, campus organizations can benefit by redesigning academic and/or administrative organizations into natural work teams. On one level, this might simply mean involving faculty or staff in team-building activities, as described in Chapter 5. On another level, it can mean formally structuring the organization into teams that will work on improving processes, measuring stakeholder satisfaction, or other vital improvement functions. Or it can mean the creation of short-term teams within an academic or administrative unit to accomplish a specific goal.

Academic units have a long history of forming natural work teams to address academic issues, such as the review and redesign of a curriculum. Search committees to fill faculty and administrative positions are another common use of teams that are created for a special purpose but that draw their membership from within the organization. In most respects, these teams will benefit from an understanding of group processes described in Chapter 5 and often will benefit from the concept of the diagnostic and remedial journey described earlier in this chapter.

Organizations may decide to challenge an existing group of employees to work as a team to improve their processes. The University of Michigan has formed numerous natural work teams that focus employees in a work group on improving their process. The facilities organization has used work groups to improve computer graphics services, customer response rates in building services, and plant building services. Other Michigan work groups have focused on establishing an alumni/donor help line, the implementation of optical imaging in the Office of Sponsored Programs, Student Loans, and Financial Operations, and improvements in property control and customer service in the Benefits Office.

The School of Dentistry at the University of Michigan developed multiple natural work teams to address a wide range of quality issues. Teams were used to develop a new patient brochure, to improve the patient billing process, to improve computer communications with departments, to improve accuracy of insurance claims, to improve the x-ray unit, to coordinate treatment in graduate clinics, to improve the patient registration process, and to improve the school's appearance and aesthetics.[8]

Administrators can also bring faculty and staff within a unit together to focus on a specific goal. The vice president in charge of the division of research at Binghamton University brought representatives from its eleven research units together to discuss issues brought about due to rapid growth, increased compliance with federal regulations, and a new line of research support services. The team met in a one-day retreat, with facilitation from the Center for Quality. In this setting, the team created a vision for the research organization's future and discussed the approaches for making changes. The team developed ideas for starting a division Web site, having a dedicated communications director, and the development of a research newsletter. This initial work by a team within the unit set the stage for a strategic planning process the following year.

STUDENT TEAMS

Belmont University has had success with organizing teams composed entirely of students to address improvement of academic programs. Belmont's student teams engage students in analyzing a course during the semester instead of waiting until the end of the semester. The activity provides better feedback to faculty and helps students take responsibility for their learning. Student teams are made of three to five students in a class who gather data, make suggestions, and assess changes in the course structure and activities. Students help redesign the organization of course materials, organize study sessions and study groups, and design buddy assignments to enhance student engagement. Over seventy faculty members at Belmont have used the student teams to improve courses.[9]

TEAMS VS. COMMITTEES

Many higher educational institutions rely on standing committees to ensure faculty and staff participation in the governance of the institution. A committee can sometimes work as a team, but committees are not necessarily teams. Teams are usually established to create change. A committee may exist to maintain balance, to protect boundaries, and to provide a forum for discussion that may or may not lead to change. Teams strive to establish consensus. Committees can focus on identifying common ground and working on consensus, or they can establish either-or conflicts, with different groups advocating different positions in a manner that creates winning and losing factions. It all depends on the leadership of the committee.

It is certainly possible for the leader of a committee to adopt the methods of a cross-functional team, to identify and prioritize issues, to collect data, and to develop strategies to improve the processes and organizations that are within the committee's scope of responsibility.

NO TEAM COOKIE CUTTERS

Although there are commonalities among cross-functional teams and among natural work teams, the fact is that every team is a unique combination of people working within the unique culture of an organization on issues that are unique to their institution. Two cross-functional teams within the same institution can work in radically different ways. Two teams at different campuses, working on similar problems with similar campus representation, can approach the same issues in different ways due to the culture of their campuses and the unique perspectives that individuals bring to teams, and both can be successful.

Beyond the broad generalization that teams tend to go through a diagnostic and a remedial journey, there is no cookie cutter approach to forming and guiding teams in an academic setting. Belmont University's Susan Williams has observed the need to create a "team mindset" whereby the process of analysis conducted by a team that may take several months to complete must replace the urge to jump in with a quick fix. Williams has observed that teams sometimes start off with assumptions about what stakeholders want, but after data collection, they sometimes discover they have significantly misunderstood their stakeholders.[10]

The campus continuous improvement initiative needs to be flexible, drawing upon a wide range of tools and methods. This is one of the reasons for establishing some form of campus office that provides expertise in team facilitation. This is also the reason to invest in training academic and administrative support leaders in a wide range of continuous improvement tools and concepts.

The staff members who support continuous improvement activities need to be prepared to help newly formed teams sort out and prioritize the issues they will address. Facilitators need to be able to advise an organization on how to collect data through measuring existing work processes, conducting focus groups, and administering surveys. Facilitators need to be able to lead a team in flowcharting or process mapping a process and to advise an organization on how to organize and conduct benchmarking. In many cases, facilitators need to be able to help teams develop fresh and creative ways to describe how systems function and how they can be improved.

EMPOWERMENT AND ENDULLMENT

Discussion of teams and teamwork usually draws people into some reflection on the degree to which people in any organization are empowered to make decisions. Many campuses experience a great deal of strain over the manner in which decisions are made, either by faculty, staff, or administrators. The formation of cross-functional teams and natural work teams empowers people to participate in the decision-making process in their organizations. The adoption of continuous improvement methods and concepts by faculty and staff for use in meetings and with standing committees likewise enhances effectiveness and further empowers people.

Empowerment can best be thought of as a state of being in which people know the boundaries within which they are free to work, and the boundaries are appropriate to their knowledge, experience, and maturity. In an empowering setting, people are engaged in making the decisions that influence the quality of their work life, the quality of the academic experience for students, and the quality of administrative services, research, and outreach activities that make up the totality of the academic setting. Empowered people have the necessary feedback, knowledge, and skills to successfully perform their research, teaching, and administrative functions. In a state of empowerment, people feel a sense of ownership and pride in their work and are recognized for the successful role they play in making their institution successful.

No one can order people on a campus to be empowered. The best that can be done is to create a system that reinforces the state of empowerment. Empowerment is not achieved by pep talks or interpersonal relations therapy. Either the system in which faculty and staff work fosters empowerment or it fosters endullment.

The opposite of empowerment on today's campus is generally not oppression. Few would argue that faculty or staff work in oppressed conditions on most campuses, although there are areas of concern regarding possible exploitation of graduate students and adjunct faculty. Most of the academic community is not oppressed, but some may be endulled. Endullment is a concept advanced by the educator Ira Shor to describe the conditions being observed in school classrooms when the educational system does not allow students to participate in the real learning process.[11] Students turn off to the teacher, just as adults can turn off to the workplace. Students learn how to do the minimum to get by, just as faculty and staff can learn how to do the minimum to get by, as their way of staying even with a system they may resent. Consider the following comparison of empowerment and endullment.[12]

Empowerment	Endullment
People are involved in making decisions.	People are told what to do.
People have appropriate boundaries.	Boundaries are too confining.
People have feedback that allows them to understand their own performance.	Feedback comes only from an authority figure, if at all.
People have a sense of ownership of their work.	People's sense of ownership is very limited.
People are proud of their work and their campus.	People are apathetic about their work and their campus.

In most organizational settings, continuous improvement efforts have the added benefit of drawing people out of a sense of endullment and toward a state of empowerment. The more authority is given to a team to diagnose and implement change, the more the team members will create a sense of empowerment. The more open the organization is to listening to stakeholders, identifying problems and opportunities, and engaging people in creating change that benefits them and their institution, the more people are drawn away from endullment and toward empowerment.

Samford University's Mark Baggett observed the empowering aspect of continuous improvement efforts among faculty members as their program evolved. Baggett found that faculty members achieved a new sense of empowerment when they discovered and learned to use the underlying data structures of their departments.[13]

TOOLS FOR TEAMS

The idea of committees and task forces has been around for decades within higher education, so what does continuous improvement bring to the campus that is new?

What continuous improvement has done is to consolidate a variety of tools, techniques, and theories that have emerged from a wide range of disciplines into a common body of knowledge. Continuous improvement gives campus teams new tools for more effective group processes in diagnosing systems, focusing group efforts, and communicating concepts and recommendations with the diverse languages of today's campus.

Process flowcharting and mapping, for example, was presented in Chapter 3. Process maps have been used effectively on a variety of campuses to improve a wide range of processes, including admissions, scholarship administration, enrollment, curriculum redesign, library operations, grant development, and many others. The cumulative improvement of specific processes has a powerful impact on improving student and alumni satisfaction, reducing costs, and freeing faculty time to concentrate on teaching and research.

Another powerful tool for diagnosing systems is the cause and effect diagram (sometimes called a fishbone diagram) developed by a leader of the Japanese Union of Scientists and Engineers, Dr. Kaoru Ishikawa.[14] Also known as Ishikawa diagrams, these drawings are used to focus the attention of a team on a specific issue and enable the complexity of a system to be captured in a highly visible format. The benefits of this tool are multifold. Participants are able to communicate more effectively by having a common, visible frame of reference, while a wide variety of concepts can be captured and explored by the team.

For example, there are many questionable assertions being offered regarding accountability in education. A notion seems to exist that students are like products on a conveyor belt and that holding teachers more accountable for student performance will result in improved performance by students on nationally standardized exams. This simplistic notion ignores the complex set of causes and effects that exists in any educational setting. The complexity of the relationship between cause and effect in education can be illustrated with an Ishikawa cause and effect diagram, as seen in Figure 8.1.

Although many parents and politicians may not want to admit it, learner motivation remains a primary factor that impacts learning outcomes. One survey of college students at The University of Alabama suggests that many take a class and have a target of a grade they want to obtain. The goal is not to make the highest grade possible, but to make a grade that meets their objectives regarding the balance between effort expended and grade that satisfies their needs. If maximized learning is not necessarily the goal of students, then the notion that performance on standardized exams is an indicator of the quality of an educational process is a house built on sand.

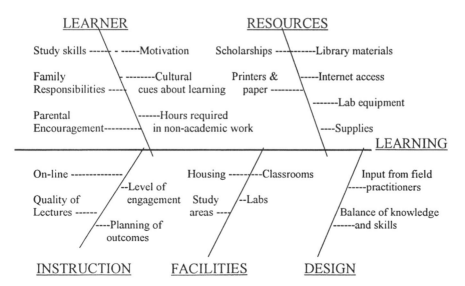

Figure 8.1 Ishikawa Cause and Effect Diagram

Campuses can also benefit from a method known as quality function deployment. Community colleges, colleges, and universities all use work systems that depend on different organizations and individuals performing different tasks at different times during a semester or year. Failure to properly execute a task on time at one part of the campus will result in significant problems later on at another location regarding student admissions, retention, graduation, and ultimately in donor support.

Flowcharts and cause and effect diagrams are powerful tools for diagnosing and clarifying roles, sequence, and importance of components of complex work processes that cross organizational boundaries and stretch out over semesters.

The quality function deployment chart is a valuable tool for capturing and sharing key work process information to enable administrators to train new staff, to plan for variations in workload that come with semesters, and to monitor processes to ensure that the right job is being performed by the appropriate people at the right time. This chart was introduced to the West by Dr. Yoji Akao, of Tamagawa University, in Tokyo, Japan.[15] A quality function deployment chart describes activities, the time they should occur, and the individual or function that should carry out the activity. Table 8.1 is a simplified version of a quality function deployment chart used by Student Support Services at The University of Alabama.

SUMMARY

Any campus can organize cross-functional teams or challenge existing work groups to improve. However, to ask people to diagnose and improve work systems without equipping them with diagnostic tools and appropriate methods for collecting data and understanding the nature of common cause and special causes of variation will result in disappointment and disillusionment among faculty, staff, and students who are misled in this manner.

On the other hand, continuous improvement is not simply a collection of tools. Although continuous improvement includes some unique tools, they cannot be used effectively apart from a philosophical framework based on the understanding of the importance of process variation and the need to be able to establish consensus and collaboration within an academic or administrative setting.

Continuous improvement efforts are certainly effective in creating teamwork within academic and administrative departments, and this is important for many types of process improvement. However, most campuses rely on a complex relationship between multiple units in order to

Table 8.1
Quality Function Deployment Chart

Activity	Start	Finish	Mgr.	AC	Counselors	Office Staff	SAB Counselor	Peer Mentor
Sign timesheets	Bi-weekly	Bi-weekly	X	X		X		X
File timesheets	Bi-weekly	Same Day				X		
Send tutor verification letter	Thursdays	As needed		X		X		
Send reminder letter	Tuesday and Thursday	As needed		X		X		
Check supply inventory	Monthly	3rd				X		
Weekly staff meeting	Thursday	As needed	X	X	X			
Enter contacts in database	Weekly	9/2		X				
Choose peer mentors for fall								X
Choose advisory board members	8/1	8/11					X	

provide vital stakeholder services. The continuous improvement methods provide effective concepts and tools to enable cross-functional teams to unravel the knotty problems that inhibit campuses from meeting and exceeding stakeholder needs. In many cases, teams need to collect and analyze data in order to improve a process, which leads us to the next chapter.

NOTES

1. Joseph Juran, *Managerial Breakthrough* (New York: McGraw Hill, 1964).

2. Ibid.

3. Donald Schon, *The Reflective Practitioner* (New York: Basic Books, 1983).

4. Center for Quality, "Orientation Team Makes Real-Time Registration a Reality," Binghamton University, *Partners*, 2 no. 1 (2001).

5. Center for Quality and Planning, *Achieving Goals*, Pennsylvania State University, November 2000.

6. Joanne Nagy, et al., "Madison: How TQM Helped Change an Admissions Process," *Change* (May/June 1993).

7. University of Miami, *Continuous Improvement Update*, March 2001.

8. M Quality, "Quality in Daily Activities," The University of Michigan, 1996.

9. Harry Hollis, "Quality Profile: Belmont University," The Conference Board, July 1997.

10. Susan Williams, "How Quality Improvement Teams Work to Improve Processes in Departments and Academic Units," in *Quality Quest in the Academic Process*. Samford University, Birmingham, AL, 1992.

11. Ira Shor, *Empowering Education* (Chicago: University of Chicago Press, 1992).

12. John R. Dew, *Empowerment and Democracy in the Workplace* (Westport, CT: Quorum Books, 1997).

13. Mark Baggett, "Demythologizing Quality Improvement for Faculty," in *Quality Quest in the Academic Process*. Samford University, Birmingham, AL, 1992.

14. Kaoru Ishikawa, *Guide to Quality Control* (Tokyo, Japan: Asian Productivity Center, 1976).

15. Yoji Akao, *Quality Function Deployment* (Cambridge, MA: Productivity Press, 1990).

CHAPTER

Measurement and Feedback

A system is like a mobile—touch one part and the whole thing moves.

—Maury Cotter, UW–Madison

There are few topics more controversial in higher education than the question of how to measure performance and effectiveness of academic programs and support processes. Academics are properly suspicious of measurement schemes that might inadvertently create adverse consequences that undermine complex learning processes.

The adage in the continuous improvement field is "What Gets Measured Is What Gets Done," and this can certainly be true in higher education. Faculty members frequently voice concerns regarding what gets measured in tenure and promotion decisions, noting that the choice of measurement criteria drives where they will devote their time.

Whenever an institution establishes a structured approach to defining and obtaining performance measures, it runs the risk of creating an engine that pulls the entire organization, like cars on a train, in a certain direction. Once the organization is hitched to the measurement engine, it may be hard to decouple, even when concerns arise about unexpected consequences of the measurement system.

The problem with measurement in higher education is that the processes and outcomes can be so varied. It is easy to create a measurement engine that fits one area, such as learning math skills, but it may be counterproductive to apply the same measures to evaluate the learning process for music.

Because of the diversity among higher education institutions, comparative measures can be deceptive and even harmful. Differences in types of academic programs, levels of commitment to research, private or state-owned status, and cost-of-living differences between regions can confound comparative measures among institutions.

Chapter 1 introduced the observation that higher educational institutions will move through several developmental phases as they refine and expand their use of the continuous improvement concepts and tools. It is natural for institutions to struggle with the establishment of effective measures and to advance through several iterations before reaching a set of measures that provides appropriately diverse feedback.

Institutions must move cautiously through several iterations to develop a set of internal and comparative measures that will provide useful information.

INPUT-PROCESS-OUTPUT

The input-process-output model, introduced in Chapter 3, provides a useful framework for discussing measurement and feedback in higher education and can be used as an initial taxonomy.

Input Measures

Any institution will have a variety of *input measures* that can be used to evaluate the overall quality of the institution. Remember that low quality in inputs will invariably result in low quality in outputs and create all manner of quality problems with internal processes.

The most widely used input measure is the score of incoming students on national standardized tests—SAT and ACT. Comparative data are also collected nationally by *U.S. News & World Report* on the percent of students in a freshman class who were in the top 10 percent and top 25 percent of their graduating high school class. Institutions may collect other input measures, such as student demographic data, student attitudes about social issues, and information regarding the terminal degrees of the faculty. Although there are examples of students with low scores on standardized tests who do well in college, and there are examples of students with high scores on standardized tests who fail at college, in general, schools compete for the students with the highest scores on standardized tests because they are perceived to be the most likely to perform well in college.

Most institutions are well versed in the average standardized test scores and the range of those scores for their students. This is valuable data for

planning academic programs and should be tracked longitudinally to observe trends. It is not uncommon for this to become an important strategic indicator for academic departments or colleges that are seeking to
increase their academic reputation.

Process Measures

Most institutions have the potential for drowning in *process measures*,
which are intended to give feedback about how well a teaching or administrative process is working. Student performance in classes, student evaluations of faculty, and student evaluations of administrative processes are
all important process measures on any campus. Faculty evaluation of support services and the peer review of academic programs are likewise critical
process measures.

Other process measures used nationally in the *U.S. News & World Report* examine the percent of classes with less than twenty students and the
percent of classes with more than fifty students at an institution, the ra-
tio of faculty to students, and the percent of faculty members who are full-
time. These are useful measure for looking at campus processes from high
altitude. However, all these measures are more insightful when a campus
uses them to examine each specific college or major academic program.

There are assumptions embedded in the measures that are used by *U.S.
News & World Report* that may not necessarily be correct. There is an as-
sumption that small classes may be better than large classes and that a
greater percentage of full-time faculty may indicate a higher quality academic program. This illustrates the swampy ground that one enters when
beginning to discuss measures in higher education.

There are so many processes on a university campus that it is easy to
move into overload with process measures. Each academic and administrative unit will need to focus on a critical few measures that provide the
most useful feedback about processes. The office that handles student financial aid will need its set of process measures, which will be different
from the set of process measures used by the chair of the English Department.

Output Measures

Output measures are more commonly thought of as outcome measures
in the language of educators and provide insight into the results of an
academic or administrative process. Output measures can include student
performance on professional examinations, feedback from employers that

hire graduates, feedback from alumni on the results of their education, the number of faculty publications, the number of faculty performances and exhibits in the arts, the number of citations of faculty, the level of funding for research, the number of patents granted, and the number of students graduated. Universities that claim teaching, research, and service in their mission will want to consider outcome measures for service activities, such as the dollar value of faculty support to regional schools, health care, and service agencies.

The six-year graduation rate is one of the most commonly used outcome measures, but it is a very poor measurement tool due to the incredible lag time between performance and output. Looking at the institution's performance from the long-term view, the six-year graduation rate is useful, but it is almost impossible to determine if a specific change or innovation impacts the six-year rate.

Some measures can be both process measures and outcome measures. The freshman retention rate is a good example. It provides very useful feedback on the outcome of the freshman year experience and is also an indicator of the total college experience as a process measure. The freshman retention rate is extremely useful because it provides educators with relatively quick feedback about changes in academic and administrative processes. Faculty can tell within a year if changes in enrollment strategies, in a core curriculum, or in how a significant class is taught have changed student performance.

There are outcome measures for many support processes that can serve as process measures for the overall institution. Alumni giving is an outcome measure of a process of developing alumni relationships. International student recruitment levels are an outcome measure of a special recruitment and enrollment process within the institution. The outcomes of specific processes can be important measures of the health of an institution.

DECIDING WHAT TO MEASURE

Many organizations have taken counterproductive approaches in their early efforts to develop performance measures. The most frequent problem is to attempt to measure everything, which leads to wasting time, resources, and wearing out lots of people.

Joseph Juran taught the concept of identifying the vital few factors that account for most of the outcomes or results in a system.[1] Many universities measure their freshman retention rate as a primary process and outcome measure, for example. In examining data related to freshman performance, there are many possible factors that can account for freshman success, such as academic preparation in high school, financial constraints, and excessive use of alcohol or drugs. The relative importance of each of these factors might differ greatly from one campus to the next. Each institution needs to decide on its vital few measures that are most important for tracking institutional performance and progress on key initiatives.

An important rule of measurement in higher education is to study a process, looking for the vital few factors, and then to establish measures of these vital few factors and to use the data to develop and assess improvements.

Each level in the organization should have an appropriate set of measures. The chancellor or president should establish an overarching set of key measures that quickly summarizes the overall health of the institution and progress in key areas.

At Samford University, in Birmingham, Alabama, the president, Thomas Corts, has established a set of ten key indicators that works well for a private university, including financial indicators, tuition, enrollment, retention rates, graduation rates, and instructional expenditures per student.[2]

While the president may track comparative data on the number of faculty as one of many indicators, the provost will also have this as one of a set of key measures that might also include the percentage of courses taught by tenure and tenure-track faculty, feedback from academic program reviews, and feedback from faculty and student surveys and focus groups concerning academic processes. Not all the key indicators for the provost will flow up to the president, but they are all important to the provost.

The same is true for the vice president of Student Affairs, who will have a different set of key measures that includes performance data related to student housing, meals, disciplinary cases, health center performance, and student recreation programs. Only one of the Student Affairs key measures may flow up to the president. The directors within each unit in Student Affairs will have their own set of performance measures. Residential Life may have a set of measures that relates to the performance and function of residence halls. Only one of these measures may flow up to the vice president for Student Affairs, and none may flow up to the president on a routine basis.

In addition to these performance measures, each administrative office and academic unit may have feedback measures that are specific to it that come from surveys and focus groups that usually would not flow up to the appropriate vice president, unless the data indicated a need and opportunity to improve a process.

The purpose of collecting all these data is to identify opportunities for improvement. If, for example, the data indicate that students and parents are unhappy with the cleanliness of the residence halls, then the institution can create a team to study the cleaning process and perhaps benchmark other institutions that have a better system in place.

Internal surveys from students, for example, helped The University of Alabama Student Health Center identify the need to reduce the amount of time that students were waiting to see a doctor. The Health Center director organized a team to collect data and to analyze the existing process and work flow and developed several ideas to shorten student wait time without adding more physicians or staff.

BALANCING MEASURES

Carl Thor, with the American Productivity and Quality Center, offered an important insight into measures.[3] Thor noted that it is easy for an organization to focus on one or two internal process measures and to become excellent in those limited areas. This is the problem associated with the "measurement engine" that pulls the organization into counterproductive situations or leads to the suboptimization of an institution's resources. An enrollment office at a university could, for example, decide that answering the telephone before it rings three times should be a vital measure and could train and reward staff for quickly answering the phone. The department could be the fastest phone answerers in all of academe. But this could have adverse results if prospective students who are visiting the campus are neglected by staff while telephones are being studiously answered, if e-mail inquiries are left unanswered, or if processing applications falls behind because of a fixation on answering the telephone.

The point is that it is relatively easy to select one thing to measure and to become very good at it, whereas success may depend on doing a variety of things well. Thor suggested that an organization should create a set of measures that provides a balanced perspective. Many organizations have found that a set of four, six, or even eight measures will provide a balanced view of organizational performance. Having too many measures can cause excessive time and resources to be spent in measuring and can lead to paralysis by analysis. Having too few measures can cause an organization to fail to pay appropriate attention to diverse areas.

This balance of measures has been likened to a dashboard on a car—a set of indicators that gives immediate feedback to the driver—or department chair, dean, or director.[4] The University of Miami has created an excellent set of "dashboards" for their administrative areas.

In some areas, this has come to be called a "balanced scorecard" that gives a balanced view of multiple input, process, and output measures. The California State University System has created the nation's best system-wide process for collecting stakeholder feedback on a wide range of administrative issues for a "balanced scorecard" that provides comparative data between institutions.

SECRET SHOPPING

Some institutions have developed "secret shopping" programs in which students go into an office to receive a service. These students have been asked to observe and record information regarding how they are treated, the responsiveness of the staff, the quality of services, and other operational information. The University of Miami has established a secret shopping process that is customized for each service area. Service area managers meet with the quality staff to identify the key service issues and measurement criteria. A plan is created to identify how to test and measure the service. Staff or students visit the service area and make their observations, and management receives feedback through the quality office.[5]

FOCUS GROUPS

Focus groups can be an important source of qualitative feedback that can be used to assess individual classes, an overall academic program, or the performance of an administrative or support function on campus. Focus groups can also be used to determine student, faculty, and staff views on specific campus issues, to identify staff and faculty training needs, and to identify questions that should be included in surveys that will provide quantitative data.

Steps in preparing and conducting a focus group are:

1. Plan how to pull together a representative group of participants for the focus group. Think about who the participants should be and what would appeal to them about participating in a focus group, and be sure to select a mix of people that adequately represents the populations whose views you wish to understand.

2. Plan the logistics for the focus group session. Timing is the most critical factor to consider. Be sensitive to the other demands on the group you are trying to reach. Do not schedule student focus groups when students are preparing for final exams. Do not schedule faculty focus groups

at the beginning or end of a semester. Do not try to conduct a focus group with the enrollment staff during their peak time for responding to student applications. Plan to conduct the focus group in a location that will be quiet and comfortable and provide some refreshments for the participants. When conducting focus groups with undergraduate and graduate students, it often helps to provide free pizza to encourage them to attend and to provide something in exchange for their help. Rutgers University offers students free "bucks" on their campus cash cards and gives students gift certificates from its bookstore. Alabama rewards participants with snacks, tee shirts, and even meals. Plan to have a flip chart stand, an easel, and plenty of markers to record the comments from the group.

3. Plan how the participants will be contacted. Decide who will contact the participants and how they will be reached. Make sure that the process includes a way to confirm whether the invited participants will actually attend. It is worthwhile to do some wordsmithing on exactly what people will be told when they are contacted and asked to participate in the focus group.

4. Plan who will facilitate the focus group and who will observe. The ideal approach is to have a person who is completely neutral conduct the focus group. If the focus group is designed to obtain student feedback about an academic program, it is best to have someone who does not teach in that program to conduct the focus group. Observers need to be few in number and restricted to observing. If observers start to question or argue with participants, the focus group will become dysfunctional. In many cases, it is effective to start the focus group with an open-ended question, asking participants to identify strengths and areas for change (pluses and deltas) about the focus group topic. If the focus group is providing feedback on an academic program, ask the students to start by identifying what they think to be the program's strengths and what they consider to be areas needing change. Keep in mind that participants will often describe the areas of strength with a broad brush ("the faculty is great") while they will describe the areas for change with a fine brush ("we need more crackers in the vending machine").

5. Prepare a list of specific follow-up questions to ask the group after they have shared their views about strengths and areas for change. In some cases, there are questions that will have already been covered by the participants as they identified strengths and areas for change. In other cases, there may be important questions that need to be posed to the group that they would not have approached on their own. For instance, students may speak up about the quality of their classes and the availability of faculty, but they may not think to volunteer information about

how they are treated by the office staff. It is important to have a clear understanding of all the areas you want to learn about from the participants and to be prepared to ask questions about each issue. Note: If the facilitator starts the focus group by asking narrowly focused questions, the participants will start to give only narrowly focused responses. They may then feel conditioned to share information only in narrow areas and may not subsequently be willing to share other concerns. Also, if the session starts with narrow issues, the participants may become distrustful and may suspect that the issues they came prepared to discuss are not going to be addressed. Therefore, it is almost always more effective to start with open-ended questions and then move to the narrow, focused questions that may cover the details that you most want to know about. Before conducting the focus group, it is important to plan how the data will be organized and reviewed. Have a clear plan as to who will transcribe the information from flip chart pages to regular paper. It may be useful to have that individual in the room with a laptop computer, collecting the information as it is generated. Binghamton University has conducted focus groups in rooms where the discussion can be videotaped for future analysis.

Be prepared for surprises. The saying is true in most organizations, "You don't know what you don't know." Focus groups often bring issues to the surface that faculty or staff did not know were concerns.

Examples

At Western Wisconsin Technical College, the president conducts focus groups with the LaCrosse community and five other communities where the college provides branch campuses. The president obtains feedback from employers, community officials, educators, and former and potential students regarding the services provided by WWTC.[6]

In preparation for a reaccreditation, the College of Social Work at The University of Alabama conducted focus groups with freshmen and sophomores; juniors; seniors; first-year Masters in Social Work (MSW) students; second year MSW students; MSW students in Mobile, Alabama; MSW students in a weekend program; and doctoral students. Each focus group began by asking the students to identify the strengths and areas for change in the academic program. The college dean and the department chairs prepared a list of specific follow-up questions that were used to ensure they received feedback on specific areas of interest. The sessions were all conducted by staff from the Office for Continuous Quality Improvement and were conducted either during class time or during required professional development sessions. Faculty members were not present during any of the sessions in order to encourage students to speak freely.

Social Work students provided very broad positive feedback regarding the knowledge of their faculty, the faculty's willingness to provide personal attention, excellent placement in community agencies for field studies, and helpfulness of office staff. They also gave detailed feedback concerning areas for change, including useful details such as needed improvements in vending machines. A verbatim report of participant feedback was prepared for review by the entire faculty and used in the opening stages of self-assessment for reaccreditation.

The Center for Quality at Binghamton University uses focus groups extensively in its work. Focus groups have proved to be excellent sources of information for one-time diagnosis as well as for ongoing assessments. Binghamton has used ongoing student focus groups to help the Decker School of Nursing and the Systems Science Graduate Program both to evaluate their publications and to develop new materials that are effective in recruiting new students.

One of the most effective focus groups at Binghamton was conducted in conjunction with the Watson School of Engineering and Applied Science. This focus group was composed of new undergraduate students and met several times a month for an entire year to evaluate the school's marketing and recruiting strategies, including publications and letters from the deans and departments. The group recommended extensive revisions in the marketing and recruiting strategies, as well as changes in the letters and publications. For example, the group revised the style, content, and length of the dean's letter to accepted freshmen. The students stated that they felt all colleges say the same thing in their letters, and they, in essence, stopped reading them after the second paragraph. Thus, new letters and publications became shorter, more visual, and contained bullets of information.

Using the focus group as the final opinion in the development of publications was a new concept both in the Watson School and on the campus. The result for the Watson School was a dramatic increase in applications, freshman yield rate, and entering freshman academic quality. The dean exhibited wisdom, courage, and humility in accepting and implementing all of the focus group's recommendations. The Center for Quality also routinely uses focus groups of parents, staff, and community people to provide data to enable the teams they are facilitating to reach better and more informed decisions and recommendations.

Focus groups are commonly used with task forces and quality improvement projects at the University of Wisconsin–Madison, as well. Among their hundreds of quality teams, Wisconsin formed a Safety Task Force in their Facilities, Planning and Management organization. Twenty team members attended workshops on conducting focus groups. The team members then facilitated thirteen focus groups on safety issues. The focus groups were conducted in shop areas, such as the sheet metal shop, the paint shop, carpentry, and vehicle service shop. Participants were asked open-ended questions to initiate the discussion: "What do you feel are the three most effective ways for you to receive safety related information? What safety-related information is most important to you?" The focus group facilitators were pleased with the amount of feedback they received and were surprised by the degree of "passion" the participants had for the topic.[7]

COMMUNITY FORUMS

In some cases, campuses use a town hall meeting to share information and receive feedback from all faculty, students, and staff about important issues. This open style of discussion builds democracy on the campus and serves as an effective model for students to learn for community leadership.

The University of Wisconsin–Stout conducts community forums that function in a manner similar to focus groups. A topic is identified, such as the budget, parking, or the campus master plan, and people from all across the campus meet to provide feedback and perspectives on the issue.[8]

SURVEYS

Surveys are extremely useful in determining stakeholder satisfaction with a wide range of processes and outcomes. Surveys can be used to obtain campuswide feedback from students, faculty, parents, staff, and other stakeholders, or can be used to obtain feedback on a very specific academic or administrative area. Campuses can participate in comparative surveys that allow them to see how they stand in relation to similar institutions or may use internally developed surveys that provide more detailed information. These are all effective ways to develop a better understanding about the effectiveness of programs and support activities.

Internal surveys are designed for specific campus organizations to determine their stakeholders' opinions about the services being provided. Internal stakeholder surveys often focus on students during the school year and parents during summer orientation sessions. Some campuses conduct an annual survey of students to determine their satisfaction with academic and administrative services, along with questions related to the campus culture and climate. Others survey the faculty, staff, and alumni.

The University of Michigan has conducted a campuswide work environment survey for noninstructional staff. Staff members have been asked their opinion about the university's orientation to change, the management style in departments, unit performance, compensation, physical environment, staff development, and planning processes. Survey results were published in a newspaper format report for everyone on campus, providing summary statistical data and interpretation of the results.[9] A similar survey process has been used at Villanova.

Western Wisconsin Technical College also conducts an annual climate survey. Data from this survey have been used for over ten years to adjust administrative processes. For example, survey feedback caused WWTC to redesign its executive committee to include middle managers and curriculum designers to increase their voice in decision making. Survey feedback led to improved communications with community groups as well.[10]

Campus organizations also develop their own surveys, such as University Police and University Libraries in order to seek feedback from students, faculty, and staff. These surveys are increasingly developed as Web-based surveys, such as a Web-based survey recently used by the Dining Services Department at Villanova. The School of Human Ecology at Penn State is another example, conducting an annual survey of its alumni.

At the University of Wisconsin–Stout, the Housing and Residential Life staff conduct an annual Quality of Life Survey.[11] Surveys for students cover issues such as the quality of classrooms, dining services, housing, recreation, parking, and health services. There is a special survey to obtain student perspectives about move-in day, and a survey that helped Food Services understand students' preferences in breakfast cereals. Stout uses the ACT Student Opinion Survey to obtain information that can be compared with student opinions at other institutions.

The internal process for developing campus surveys should include the following steps.

1. Organize a cross-functional team that will prepare the survey questions. The team members need to represent all the organizations on campus that are seeking information from the survey. The team's job is to define what their organizations want to learn from their stakeholders through this survey. In designing surveys for faculty and academic administrators, the design team may conduct focus groups with faculty and department chairs to help determine which questions were appropriate for each group.

The person who is responsible for establishing the team that will design the survey would do well to include a faculty member who has experience in survey design.

The survey design team must balance out the question of maintaining the anonymity of respondents with the ability to cross-tabulate the data in order to focus on concerns of specific groups on campus. For example, it might be wonderful to ask faculty members who respond to a survey to identify their academic department in order to compare responses from one department to the next, but if the demographics also include information on gender or years at the institution, faculty members can easily perceive that the detail of the demographics could make it possible for their responses to be identified individually, and they may be reluctant to respond.

If the survey team wants to be able to break out data into smaller subgroupings, it is important to collect a very large sample so that the size of the subgroupings will be significant. For example, a random sample of 150 students may provide useful information about a campus with 3,000 students, but attempting to break the responses of 150 into smaller groups, such as comparing responses of chemistry majors to art majors, would not be sound.

2. After the team has developed the survey instrument, the team should develop a plan for conducting the survey. In some cases, a survey can be administered to an entire population, such as everyone who lives in a particular residence hall. In most cases, however, the team will need to develop a method to administer the survey to a random sample of the overall population. Care must be taken to ensure that the sample used in the survey is not skewed in some direction.

3. With a draft of the survey instrument in hand, and a plan for conducting the survey in place, it is time to seek a fresh set of eyes to review the survey and the surveying plan. The team should find a faculty member who teaches surveying methods to critique the survey and the sampling plan.

4. Administer the survey and collect the results. It is important to have a powerful statistical software package available for analyzing the results. Survey results can be used in a variety of ways. It is often useful to write a summary report to be circulated among deans, department chairs, administrative leaders, and student leaders. It is important to have a group identified who will spend some time examining the data to ask, "So what?"

5. In some cases, data from a survey lead to the formation of teams or task forces to address a problem. In other cases, information from surveys helps in developing long-range plans. At Alabama, for instance, survey information from faculty included a question about satisfaction with

parking. When the data were cross-tabulated by college surveyors, it became clear as to which part of the campus was experiencing parking problems and which part had adequate parking. In some cases, survey data may lead to questions for a follow-up survey. A survey of students in 2000 led to a follow-up survey in 2001 that asked more specific questions about student concerns with the scheduling and availability of classes.

In some cases, it will be beneficial to have a common survey question that is used in a variety of surveys of different stakeholder populations. This creates the opportunity to understand how different stakeholders might perceive an issue. Parents, for example, rate Alabama's residence halls and food services higher than the students rate them. Alumni, students, and parents all give Alabama high marks for the strength of its academic programs.

COMPARATIVE SURVEYS

Internal surveys allow an institution to understand how its stakeholders view a wide range of issues. However, in many cases it is useful to be able to compare the perspectives of an institution's stakeholders with the perspectives of stakeholders at similar institutions. This is an extremely tricky process.

The problem with most comparative surveys in higher education is that they compare apples with oranges. It does not help a small college to see comparative data from large universities, or vice versa. Data that mix public and private institutions are flawed from the start. Comparisons between similar institutions in different regions of the country can also be misleading. Is there any hope?

There are approaches to developing useful comparative data that can be pursued. The California State University System, for example, has identical stakeholder surveys that are used at all their campuses to obtain feedback in administrative areas. This can be useful, as long as people keep in mind that there is still a great deal of variation in settings between campuses in various parts of such a large state.

The most useful approach is to collect comparative data from similar institutions with the help of a neutral party, such as a regional accrediting body. Comparative data from the Southern University Group, for example, allows schools in the region to compare data with other similar state institutions.

However, there is something to be said for comparative data from dissimilar institutions. Large universities can and should learn best practices from small private colleges. Institutions on the West Coast can learn best practices from institutions in the Mid-west, and vice versa. A breakthrough in teaching freshman mathematics is a breakthrough that can be applied in any higher educational setting. A best practice in operating a career center can work in any part of the country.

The University of Wisconsin–Stout has made significant gains using feedback from the ACT Alumni Survey, the ACT Student Opinion Survey, and the National Survey of Student Engagement. Each of these surveys provides useful information about the institution's performance from the stakeholders' perspective and also provides valuable comparative data.

Institutions must always come back to the question of why they want to collect comparative data. Is it to develop some degree of assurance that they are running in the middle of the pack and can be comfortable, or is it to seek out best practices that can be honorably adopted to lead to continuous improvement of all academic and administrative processes?

It is certainly useful to have comparative snapshots, detailed comparative data, on a wide range of process measures, even from dissimilar institutions. Comparative costs of course offerings, comparative data on course size, and comparative use of tenured and adjunct faculty to teach courses can be valuable to an institution.

The Baldrige Criteria for Higher Education encourages colleges and universities to seek comparative data. As a result of the emphasis on comparative outcomes, many schools are starting to use the National Survey for Student Engagement and the ACT Alumni Outcomes survey.

COMMENT AND FOLLOW-UP FEEDBACK

Feedback systems provide another source of measurement. A system for obtaining feedback can range from a simple device, such as a comment card used in a food court to provide feedback on meals and services, to a more comprehensive system of feedback regarding student views about courses.

Institutions handle student feedback on courses, for example, in a variety of ways. Most go to great lengths to ensure anonymity of student comments. In some cases, student feedback is private, going directly to the faculty member. In other cases, administrators see summaries of the feedback that faculty receives. In some cases, student feedback information is summarized and posted on a Web site for all students to see. Each of these approaches poses problems and opportunities. Care must be taken to focus student feedback on the effectiveness of the faculty in teaching, clarity of assignments, adequacy of faculty feedback in grading papers and reports, and not on how hard the course materials may have been or how tough the professor was in grading.

Some institutions construct feedback systems for service organizations by using a "secret shopper" methodology. Students are provided with a list of services to evaluate in an office. They call or visit the office with a legitimate and reasonable request and evaluate how well the office staff responded to their question. In these cases, students look for accuracy of information, timeliness of response, and courtesy of the office staff.

LONGITUDINAL DATA

It is very important to consider the example in Chapter 6 regarding the data being used to evaluate international student enrollment. Examining a snapshot of data—whether from a one-time survey, one semester's course feedback, or as information from a single focus group—can be misleading.

In some situations, data only take on meaningful significance when viewed in the context of trends and patterns of variation over time. One year's data on how parents view the quality of the academic program at an institution has some value. Data from five years allow the institution to determine if parents' views are consistent or changing over time. It is not enough to know parents' views about the academic program in one year. The institution needs to know if those views are improving, declining, or holding steady. These are vital questions that require a great deal of hard work to answer.

This implies that an institution cannot establish a set of measures and in one year have a sound understanding of its situation. The collection of data is a long-term commitment based on a philosophical understanding that the data, over time, will create profound knowledge about the performance of the institution.

For example, faculty members in a department may be upset if another faculty member leaves and is not replaced. They may think it is an outrage and an indication that the number of faculty members is decreasing. However, a review of the overall faculty numbers over several years may show an upward trend in faculty numbers for the institution, as a whole. Additions may have been made in other departments to respond to changing enrollment needs. Without the data, how can one tell what is actually happening?

SYSTEMATIC, STRUCTURED ASSESSMENT

Many organizations have worked hard to collect useful data and may have collected data over enough years to have a valuable longitudinal perspective. Even when data has been collected it is still possible, even probable, that the data will not be used to generate profound knowledge about the institution. The raw data does not become knowledge without some formal, structured approach to analyzing it. In too many cases, valuable data in higher education is only reviewed by the academic administrators. The faculty and staff committees do not see the data, so when good decisions are made (based on the appropriate use of data), faculty and staff are still baffled and offended by the decisions because they never saw the information on which the decision was based.

So, it is important for the data collection process to be formally tied to the governance process that provides a formal structure process for review of data and for faculty and staff involvement in discerning what the data means. Providing useful data to the committees that are, in theory, supposed to help govern the institution will be a novel way to improve the performance of these committees.

BALANCED SCORECARDS

It can be useful to prepare an institutional scorecard that summarizes stakeholder feedback on a variety of issues. Scorecards can either provide numerical feedback to organizations regarding how stakeholders perceive their services, or they can be translated into a slightly more qualitative approach, familiar to most faculty and students—the A, B, C, D, F continuum.

Use of the alphabetic grading continuum has a certain poetic justice within the academic environment. The institution grades the students on their performance, so why shouldn't students, faculty, alumni, staff, and parents likewise be able to grade the institution?

The University of California–Berkeley has developed a sophisticated set of balanced scorecards used in its financial affairs area. Berkeley has developed separate balanced scorecards for each of its fifty frontline work units. Each work unit's metrics consist of a few standard metrics common to all work units and other metrics that are unique to that group. Some of the standard metrics include internal employee satisfaction survey results, the group's budgetary performance, and customer survey feedback data.[12]

California State University–Chico has a balanced scorecard for the university, for Academic Affairs and for each college in Academic Affairs. The process starts with college-level performance indicators. The College of Communications, for example, has twenty-three key measures. These flow up as comparative measures for all the colleges in the Academic Affairs balanced scorecard. In this way, performance at the college level is linked with performance at the university level.[13]

The University of Alabama compiled survey feedback from students, parents, alumni, faculty, and staff to provide a report card on a variety of processes and services. Again, it is important to develop a longitudinal perspective on the report card information and to have a structured, systematic way to review the data and to determine how to take actions.

Universities that are part of a system have the opportunity to develop comparative report card data. The California State University System, for example, collects stakeholder survey data that can be compared among multiple campuses on topics such as parking, police services, and purchasing.

LINKING STRATEGIC PLANS, TEAMS, AND MEASURES

It is very important to ask how the institution's self-assessment process, strategic planning process, selection of measures, and formation of teams can be woven together into a cogent system, making a whole fabric that serves the institution.

While this can be a cyclical process, it is often best to start with the self-assessment process. The institution should conduct a self-assessment, using the criteria of a management system, like the Baldrige criteria, to identify areas where the management system needs to be improved. Then, moving into strategic planning, the institution should identify key strategic issues it needs to take, both to strengthen the management system and to accomplish vital institutional goals. Action plans should be developed to specify how strategic initiatives will be accomplished. Measures should be established to evaluate the progress on the key strategic issues and should be developed for each work group to provide useful feedback to faculty and staff. Actions should be taken based on data. Then, teams can be organized to collect and assess data and to work on process improvements.

Pennsylvania State University has recently combined the strategic planning, continuous improvement, and institutional assessment functions into one unit in order to support the overall management system for the campus. With this merger, Penn State has created an integrated planning, assessment, and improvement model that harnesses quantitative and qualitative data to drive the continuous improvement process.[14]

THE NEED FOR TENSION

Dynamic tension is normal and healthy in most organizations. The institution's goal may be to increase research, but faculty members may feel their course loads are too great to provide adequate time for research. This is not the sign of a dysfunctional organization but is, instead, a normal part of the change process.

Although some people get angry when they are asked to work toward new goals while the organization does not seem to provide adequate support to do so, anger does not resolve the issue. What is needed are teamwork and collaboration, some creative thinking, and the collection and analysis of data to develop win-win ideas.

SUMMARY

The goal is to move the campus from accomplishing random, isolated, and occasional improvements toward a more systematic approach that yields frequent improvements all across the campus. No campus can adopt a management system that provides continuous and frequent improvement in a short amount of time. There is no instant pudding, as Deming said. Creating a culture and system of continuous improvement requires the growth of capacities on campus for data collection, formal mechanisms for diagnosing the data, teamwork, strategic planning, and systematic analysis of results. It may take seven to ten years to truly change a campus culture so that it embraces continuous quality improvement, but this journey is critical to long-term success in higher education.

NOTES

1. Joseph Juran, *Managerial Breakthrough* (New York: McGraw-Hill, 1964).

2. Thomas Corts and James C. Eck, "Ten Ways to Track Performance," *Trustee Magazine* (January 2002): 14–18.

3. Carl Thor, "A Complete Organizational Measurement System," *International Productivity Journal* (Spring 1990): 21–26.

4. Christopher Meyer, "How the Right Measures Help Teams Excel," *Harvard Business Review* (May–June 1994): 95–103.

5. The University of Miami Quality Website, "Secret Shopping," April 2002.

6. Lee Rasch, "Quality . . . The Western Way," NCCI Conference, 2002.

7. Kathleen Paris, "Safety Task Force Conducts Focus Groups," Penn State Ex Change (November/December 1999).

8. Bob Johnson, "Process Management at UW-Stout," NCCI Conference, 2002.

9. "Survey Results: Perceptions of the Work Environment at Michigan," The University of Michigan, 1995.

10. Lee Rasch, "Quality . . . The Western Way," NCCI Conference, 2002.

11. Bob Johnson, "Process Management at UW–Stout," NCCI Conference, 2002.

12. Ron Coley and Paul K. Diamond, "A Balanced Scorecard for Business and Administrative Services at the University of California, Berkeley," in *Pursuing Excellence in Higher Education* (San Francisco: Jossey-Bass, 2004).

13. Quality Improvement Newsletter for the California State University System, April 2000.

14. "Center Changes Name" *Quality Endeavors* no. 72 (March/April 2003).

CHAPTER 10

Engaging Faculty and Students in Improving the Teaching and Learning Processes

Education is a learning process in which the learner, not the subject being studied, is of most importance.

—Peter Jarvis

Although the concepts and tools of continuous improvement certainly add value to the overall management system for academic and administrative processes, they can also add substantial value through engaging faculty and students in improving the teaching and learning processes.

One must be immediately cautious and avoid any temptations to over-simplify teaching and learning into some process model. Learning can occur through a wide range of processes, such as direct experience, memorization, experimentation, critical thinking, and reflective practice. Learning methods can engage many combinations of visual, audio, tactile, and even olfactory senses. There can be no simple model for the continuous improvement of teaching and learning.

However, continuous improvement practitioners in higher education began to explore the application of continuous improvement theory and methods in the classroom learning setting from introduction in the early 1990s.

Jim B. Wallace, a former quality facilitator for Southern Polytechnic State University in Marietta, Georgia, which received one of the early IBM total quality grants, observed: "The way to help more students achieve success is not to lower the standards; rather, it is to improve the educational process and thus reduce or eliminate the barriers to learning."[1]

Early advocates of continuous improvement principles and methods in college classrooms have included faculty at Samford University, Loyola University in New Orleans, and North Carolina State University, along with Southern Polytechnic State University in Georgia.

IMPROVING ACADEMIC PROGRAMS

Fisher and Weyman, at Loyola in New Orleans, have developed an overall continuous improvement model for improving curriculum in an academic program that they have applied at the graduate school level.[2] The process involves the formation of a team of faculty members, students, representatives of employers in a discipline, and other experts to improve the process. The team will use questionnaires to obtain student input and to reflect on, and enhance, the mission and vision for the academic program. A second questionnaire is then issued to students and employers to define the specific skills and abilities that graduates from the program need. The team takes the feedback and uses an affintizing process to organize the feedback into categories that can range up to as many as fifteen specific needs. Faculty, students, and alumni then participate in a process to rank the relative importance of the skills, and the team organizes a final list of topics that need to be organized as specific courses. This list of courses, which provides details of the knowledge and skills to be developed in each course, is reviewed by students, alumni, and employers for validation prior to the development of the specific courses by the faculty. Figure 10.1 illustrates the process.

A similar model was proposed by Felder and Brent at North Carolina State University.[3] Both models focus on the concept of establishing a clear process that can be managed by the academic unit in reviewing the overall content of an academic program. These process models build in several steps for ensuring the validity of the content by engaging outside experts, employers who hire and supervise graduates from the program, and alumni, who can all critique the proposed content.

This is not to marginalize the expert knowledge of the faculty members who devote their lives to the study of a discipline but to broaden the perspective of the skills and knowledge to ensure that students will be fully prepared to enter their discipline.

Although this process has benefits for undergraduate and graduate programs that are preparing students for professions, it may be argued that it does not add value to preparing students for noncareer subjects in the

```
┌─────────────────────────────────────────────┐
│ Team is formed, consisting of faculty,       │
│ students, employer representatives, and      │
│ other experts.                               │
└─────────────────────────────────────────────┘
                      ↓
┌─────────────────────────────────────────────┐
│ Students are surveyed to obtain their views  │
│ about the mission and vision of the program. │
└─────────────────────────────────────────────┘
                      ↓
┌─────────────────────────────────────────────┐
│ Team reviews student responses and uses this │
│ input to develop or refine a mission and a   │
│ vision statement for the program.            │
└─────────────────────────────────────────────┘
                      ↓
┌─────────────────────────────────────────────┐
│ A second questionnaire goes to students and  │
│ employers to identify specific knowledge,    │
│ skills and abilities needed in this field.   │
└─────────────────────────────────────────────┘
                      ↓
┌─────────────────────────────────────────────┐
│ The team affinitizes responses into          │
│ categories, each ranging up to 15 specific   │
│ needs.                                       │
└─────────────────────────────────────────────┘
                      ↓
┌─────────────────────────────────────────────┐
│ Faculty and other experts in the field rank  │
│ the categories.                              │
└─────────────────────────────────────────────┘
                      ↓
┌─────────────────────────────────────────────┐
│ Team organizes the final topics that will be │
│ covered into courses.                        │
└─────────────────────────────────────────────┘
                      ↓
┌─────────────────────────────────────────────┐
│ Listing of courses (including knowledge,     │
│ skills, and abilities) is circulated to      │
│ students, alumni, and employers for          │
│ validation.                                  │
└─────────────────────────────────────────────┘
                      ↓
┌─────────────────────────────────────────────┐
│ Faculty prepare the specific courses that    │
│ will cover the topics.                       │
└─────────────────────────────────────────────┘
```

Figure 10.1   Process for Improving an Academic Program

liberal arts. However, for undergraduate programs in the liberal arts, the faculty team may call upon graduate faculty members in their discipline to serve as "employers" who will provide feedback about the knowledge, skills, and abilities needed for graduate work. In graduate programs, faculty members may call upon department chairs at institutions that hire their graduate students as new faculty to obtain an external perspective concerning knowledge, skills, and abilities that should be covered in an academic program.

Samford University's Orlean Bullard Beeson School of Education and Professional Studies launched a continuous improvement process for its academic program in 1993.[4] Faculty members conducted a series of focus groups with their recent graduates to determine the areas in which these new teachers felt well prepared or underprepared for K–12 classroom teaching. The Samford Education faculty also conducted interviews with the principals at the schools where the majority of their graduates were placed as new teachers. The principals were asked to critique the preparation of the new teachers for work in the classroom. After reviewing the feedback, the faculty members concluded that, in spite of their best intentions, graduating teachers were still not prepared for certain aspects of classroom management. Based on this realization, the faculty organized a major redesign of the course curriculum. Subsequent focus groups with new graduates and school administrators showed a significant improvement in the preparation and performance of the new teachers.

Professional associations in a wide range of academic disciplines are likewise adopting a continuous improvement model to encourage faculty members to engage in analysis and improvement of their academic programs. The Modern Language Association (MLA), for example, has adopted a self-study methodology that employs surveys for faculty in graduate programs and graduate students to complete to provide assessment data. The MLA surveys include questions regarding faculty values and attitudes, clarity of goals of the graduate program, the relationship between generalized and specialized education in the discipline, priorities regarding preparation to conduct research, teaching in four-year colleges, teaching in two-year colleges, and teaching in secondary schools. The MLA surveys provide perspectives from within the academic unit but do not drive the faculty to obtain perspectives from alumni and other campuses that may hire their graduates.

The Accreditation Board for Engineering and Technology (ABET) has also prepared a methodology for faculty members to study their academic programs. The ABET model provides a two-loop process for evaluation and assessment of an academic program. One loop is an external process that requires the department to obtain input from its con-stituencies (primarily employers that hire their graduates). Input from these constituents is used to determine educational objectives. Faculty members then evaluate the degree to which these objectives are met in the program. The second loop draws upon the educational objectives that are identified by the constituents and develops them into knowl-edge and skill outcomes that must be achieved by the program. Faculty members determine how these outcomes will be achieved and how they will be assessed. Departmental indicators are established to measure the achievement of the educational outcomes. With this structure in place, students are engaged in educational programs, and the outcomes are evaluated.

Although this process sounds relatively simple, it actually engages fac-ulty in a very serious on-going analysis and discussion of the curriculum. Some institutions use a green-yellow-red system to indicate the department's performance in achieving educational outcomes. Outcomes that are effectively met receive a green indicator. Outcomes that need some improvement are graded as yellow. Outcomes that are not being adequately met are identified by a red indicator. When a course receives a red indicator, a defined corrective action process is used to ensure that the responsible faculty members take actions that will correct the prob-lems with a course.

IMPROVING SPECIFIC CLASSES

Although it is important to have a defined process for assessing and improving an academic program, it is also important to develop methods that faculty can use to enhance teaching and learning in specific classes.

There is already a great deal of research and literature on specific meth-ods that can be used to improve classroom learning. Some institutions are investing heavily in technology for enhanced lectures and presentations. Others are opting for problem-based learning methods that engage stu-dents in active inquiry that leads to learning outcomes. Some institutions have chosen the reading of "great books" to stimulate critical thinking, while others are engaging students in service-learning projects.

Continuous improvement methods do not focus on the specific ap-proach that a campus may select for improving learning but emphasize the formation and use of a systematic approach to evaluating and con-tinuously improving the learning process.

Samford University was again a leader in recognizing the need to focus on developing a process for evaluating and improving learning that would move beyond the normal end-of-class evaluation form. Evaluations at the end of a class provide feedback that comes too late in the process to be of any value. To provide feedback in a more timely manner, Samford faculty members developed a process model for course refinement called LEARN.[5]

In Samford's LEARN model, students are encouraged to work with faculty to provide timely feedback and suggestions during an on-going course. Early in a semester, a team of students who are taking a course together will develop a survey that they administer to fellow students regarding the course. The students summarize the data and meet with the instructor to provide feedback and ideas for changes for the course. This process allows a faculty member to make modifications to the course early during the semester in order to address problems that students may have with the teaching methodology.

This process requires students to obtain experience in developing and analyzing surveys that can provide some very useful feedback. Generally, these surveys use a Likert-type response scale that provides feedback on a wide range of issues, such as whether learning objectives are provided for each class, the usefulness of handouts, the organization of lectures, the effectiveness of class discussions and case studies, the effectiveness of visual aids, the adequacy of time for questions, the effectiveness of homework assignments and out-of-class projects, the use of the text book, the use of Web and library resources, and the effectiveness of laboratory assignments.

This process does not dictate solutions to a faculty member, nor does it require faculty members to lower their standards in any way. It does provide the faculty members with timely feedback that can correct a problem with how a fundamental concept might have been presented. It also provides faculty members with feedback that can be very useful in assessing how well students were prepared for courses when they entered an academic program, which can be valuable information to use in redesigning foundation courses or can be passed on to high school faculty.

The point of this process is for faculty members to take accountability for the learning process in their classroom and to identify problems that exist, either with their teaching methods or with the preparation of their students, and to take appropriate corrective actions. This process provides faculty members with an opportunity to engage in reflection on their teaching methods, to engage in dialog with their faculty peers, and to initiate changes that will result in improved teaching and learning.

ACADEMIC AUDITS

The University of Missouri System has piloted a process of "academic audits" to foster critical reflection among faculty about teaching. William Massey has reported on the system's efforts to create an internal process that stimulates reflection and discussion about teaching among faculty.[6]

The process encourages faculty members to reflect on how they organize their classes, what data they use to gauge their effectiveness in teaching, and how they can make the best use of campus resources. This is not a random activity but rather an organized effort to create structured discussions among faculty members about their teaching.

In the academic audit process, faculty members reflect on how their courses relate to the institution's mission. The process encourages faculty members to explore the outcomes of a course in terms of what students will be able to do and understand. Faculty members also consider how a course will build on and contribute to students' understanding of a body of knowledge. In this process, faculty members reflect on how their teaching will prepare students for a profession or for a successful life.

It is important to note that this is a process conducted by faculty and for faculty and is not driven by external interests.

IMPROVING TEACHING AS A CROSS-FUNCTIONAL PROJECT

Although improving teaching can be approached by individual faculty members working on their own classes and by faculty members in a department who want to create or improve a curriculum, it can also be approached as a cross-functional, campuswide process. Faculty can be encouraged to form a cross-functional team that will engage in a conversation and take actions to improve teaching on an entire campus.

Faculty members at one research university organized an Excellence in Teaching team that brought faculty from several colleges and libraries together to analyze and address problems in classroom teaching. This team has organized an annual Excellence in Teaching Week that provides seminars and workshops for faculty and graduate students to attend on a wide range of subjects related to teaching, such as "Race, Class, and Gender in the Classroom," "Using Library Assignments to Teach Critical Thinking Skills," "Using Web-Supplemented Course Materials," and "Effectively Teaching Large Lecture Classes."[7]

This same team undertook an assessment of their campus culture regarding teaching by using Kurt Lewin's force field analysis method.[8] The team identified forces that supported improvement in teaching and forces

Table 10.1
Acknowledging, Using, and Valuing Excellence in Teaching

Supporting Forces	Resisting Forces
Tenure and promotion system	Tenure and promotion system
Merit Raises and Rewards	Merit Raises and Rewards
	It is not really normal to talk about our teaching.
	Faculty activity reports do not provide much emphasis on teaching.
Some library resources exist.	Many journals and books on effective college teaching are not in the library.
Condition of some classrooms encourages faculty to use technology in classrooms.	Condition of some classrooms discourages use of technology.

that resisted improvement in teaching, and then developed a set of actions to be taken that would strengthen the supporting forces and weaken
the resisting forces. Table 10.1 summarizes some of the forces that the faculty members identified.

It is important to note that some forces on a campus can both support
and resist change, depending on the subculture of specific departments.
One department chair may use merit raises and rewards to reinforce and
encourage improvement in teaching, while another department chair may
ignore this issue entirely when deciding on raises and rewards.

A cross-functional team working on improving teaching may want to
benchmark other campuses or participate in national programs and discussions regarding improving teaching and learning. The Carnegie Foundation has organized the Carnegie Academy for the Scholarship of
Teaching and Learning, which provides a valuable framework in which
faculty members can address teaching issues on their own campus while
participating in a national discussion about effective teaching.

DIALOGUE WITH STUDENTS

Faculty can also engage students in an on-going discussion about effective teaching and learning with the context of a specific campus. As
part of the Excellence in Teaching project mentioned earlier, faculty and
students participated in discussion groups that provided for better mutual

understanding and the emergence of new ideas about effective teaching practices.

In one session, students shared their views about the faculty member and the student's responsibilities in the learning process. In this activity, students suggested that faculty responsibilities to student and the classroom included:

1. Availability: Good contact information and regular office hours;
2. Staying up-to-date in their field;
3. Having some understanding about the complexity of students' lives;
4. Being attentive to communication issues: avoiding jargon, looking for good analogies, self-consciously working to become a better communicator, being aware of your limitations in command of English;
5. Providing feedback. Making sure students are aware when they are in academic trouble and offering help before it is too late;
6. Being excited about your work. Not becoming complacent and not doing the same thing in class every day;
7. Respecting students—speaking to them as adults;
8. Making tests and other means of evaluation consistent with the learning in the classroom.

While providing this perspective about faculty responsibilities toward learning, students also suggested the following student responsibilities to faculty and the classroom:

1. Respect: being present, punctual, attentive, and ready to learn;
2. Being prepared: completing reading, bringing the right material to class, being aware of where you are in the syllabus;
3. Offering feedback: if something is not going well in class, speaking up about it;
4. Completing all assignments on time, consistent with the task given, and respecting all rules of academic honesty;
5. Studying appropriately: not falling behind; seeking assistance;
6. Knowing your instructors; recognizing them as complicated individuals who have their ups and downs;
7. Actively participating in class discussions and activities;
8. Being considerate of other students.
9. Pushing the professor: asking hard questions, taking advantage of resources provided.

This type of open discussion can raise the level of student and faculty awareness of teaching issues and can help make discussion of teaching a more common activity among faculty.

UNDERSTANDING STUDENT BEHAVIORS

On some campuses, there is little understanding of the complex forces at work that influence student attendance and performance in classes. Faculty may go to a great deal of effort to prepare classes but find that many students do not attend. Faculty members often have a wide variety of opinions about this problem but little data to confirm or disprove their opinions.

One public institution encountered a problem with student attendance in classes and sought to collect some data. The first attempt at data collection was to organize a focus group for students who were known for not attending class. No one showed up.

The second attempt was the design of a survey that was distributed during several different large freshman classes. Based on the survey data, the institution observed that students tend to fall into three categories regarding attendance. There is a relatively small group (about 20 percent) that never miss a class. Another group (about 40 percent) have relatively good attendance, but will miss up to four classes a semester, primarily due to sickness or personal problems. A third group (about 40 percent) claim to miss four or more classes in a semester, with some claiming to miss as many as fifteen classes. These students with high absenteeism cited the following reasons, in rank order, for skipping classes:

1. The class is offered too early in the morning for me;
2. The instructor reads from the book and I can read it for myself;
3. I can get the grade I want without attending lectures;
4. I've got to focus on other classes that are more important to me or that are harder classes;
5. I can get the information from others in my class;
6. I skip classes when I've been partying hard;
7. I had to skip classes due to a serious illness;
8. I work part-time and am tired from the work and class load;
9. The material was covered in high school.

Most freshmen with poor attendance do not think it will hurt their grades. (It does.) Freshmen with poor attendance report skipping more than one class excessively. Beginning with these behaviors as a freshman, a general pattern of poor attendance emerges. Survey data from a large class of seniors suggests that students acquire their attendance habits in the freshman year and maintain those habits through their college career, if they do not drop out.

Attendance was not influenced by expectations to attend graduate school. The only remarkable difference between freshman and upperclassmen attendance was the increased use of a "wolf pack" approach for sharing information with other students so they could miss class. Clearly, this is a learned behavior.[9]

The students' feedback regarding their ability to obtain the grade they wanted without attending class supported a theory put forth by a faculty member that, when he would work hard to improve the delivery of a class, some students would not maintain the same level of effort and obtain a higher grade but would do less work to obtain the same grade. Some students are proving to be pragmatic capitalists—seeking the maximum return on the minimum investment.

Obtaining these data did a great deal to enliven faculty interest in teaching issues and to challenge faculty to discuss the implications of the students' feedback.

THE AFFINITY PROCESS

Several references have been made to affinitizing information that is obtained through surveys of students, employers, faculty, and alumni. The affinity process is used to organize a wide range of information into logical groupings. This process is best conducted by a representative team, such as a faculty team, who are responsible for the review of an academic program.

In its low-technology form, the affinity process requires a set of Post-It notes and a large blank wall. Knowledge, skills, and abilities that are listed by faculty, alumni, or employers are each placed on a Post-It note. The faculty members place the notes on the wall and begin a silent process of organizing the notes into groups. Everyone on the team should participate. This process may take some time, since it requires everyone to read all the notes and to participate in the grouping process. Notes may be moved many times by different participants until a consensus is reached regarding the categories.

Steps in using the affinity process are:

1. Assemble an appropriate mix of participants. (For a curriculum study this might include faculty, graduates who are now working in the field, and leaders in the profession.)

2. State the objective of the exercise. Each individual works alone, writing his or her ideas on Post-It notes. There should be no discussion during this time.

3. Everyone works together to organize the notes into groupings—sometimes called buckets or piles—by positioning and repositioning the notes on a large wall.

4. When all participants are satisfied with the organization of the groupings, document the groupings. (Write it down.)

5. Plan how to address each major grouping of issues.

INTERRELATIONSHIP DIAGRAMS

Once faculty have agreed on the categories in which knowledge, skills, and abilities should be organized, it may be useful to create an interrelationship diagram to establish a common understanding as to how these categories relate to each other. In many subjects, it is highly desirable to identify foundational knowledge and skills that should be mastered by students before they move on to more advanced areas. The interrelationship diagram helps by providing a visual relationship among knowledge and skill areas that lends itself to sequencing topics and organizing lower and upper division courses (see Figure 10.2).

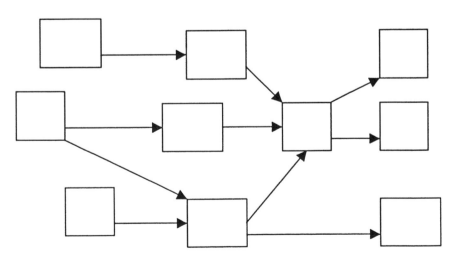

Figure 10.2   Interrelationship Diagram

OUTCOME ASSESSMENTS

Whether due to the adoption of continuous improvement methods by professional accreditation organizations, by regional accreditation groups, or from internal campus interest in improvement, more and more campuses are discussing outcome assessments.

A wide variety of outcome assessments is gaining use in various disciplines. Student surveys and exit interviews are providing excellent feedback on many campuses. The growing use of student portfolios on many campuses is providing concrete evidence of the outcome of students' participation in the college learning environment. In some cases, performance on standardized examinations is providing useful outcome data.

From a continuous improvement perspective, particularly from the management system concepts that make up the Malcolm Baldrige National Quality Award, the challenge for educators is to obtain outcome data that are comparative in nature. While it is valuable to know how well students in a program evaluate that program, it is even more valuable to know how these evaluations stack up to feedback from similar institutions.

Fortunately, two organizations have been hard at work for several years to develop feedback instruments that can provide this type of comparative feedback through the National Survey of Student Engagement (NSSE) and the ACT Alumni Outcome Survey.

The NSSE survey obtains student feedback at the freshman- and senior-year level regarding their experience in educational practices that are linked to learning and development. Students provide feedback regarding the level of academic challenge in their program (which examines items such as class preparation, course readings, written papers and reports, and course emphasis on analysis, synthesis, and judgment related to the subject matter), active and collaborative learning (including items on classroom activities such as making presentations, working on class projects, providing tutoring, and working on community-based projects), student and faculty interactions (including discussions with faculty, faculty feedback, research projects, and discussing career plans), enriching educational experiences (such as cocurricular activities, community service, independent study, foreign language study, use of technology), and a supportive campus environment (which includes support in succeeding academically, socially, and in developing relationships with students, faculty and staff).

Institutions that participate in the NSSE study receive feedback that compares their institutions with all other institutions that participate in the study and with institutions in their Carnegie classification.

The ACT Alumni Outcome Survey provides feedback on a wide set of academic issues on campus and gives institutions comparative data from a set of similar institutions. The ACT Alumni Outcome Survey provides a campus with feedback regarding educational outcomes, such as developing original ideas; thinking objectively about beliefs, attitudes, and values; defining and solving problems; recognizing and using effective verbal communication skills; analyzing and drawing conclusions from various types of data; and working cooperatively in groups. Institutions can also receive comparative feedback on other aspects of campus life, such as faculty availability to students outside of class time; ethnic, political, and religious understanding and acceptance; and personal safety on campus. The survey also provides comparative feedback on issues such as course availability, quality of instruction, class size, multicultural content of courses, condition of buildings and grounds, library services, academic advising, and other administrative processes.

SUMMARY

Continuous improvement methods add value to higher education institutions through the formation of a systematic approach to managing the institution. Through continuous improvement, institutions develop structured methods for strategic planning and assessment of outcomes. Continuous improvement methods contribute to faculty and staff engagement in teams that improve specific classes, academic programs, and administrative processes. Continuous improvement is particularly useful in addressing knotty campus problems that require collaboration of various organizations from across the campus for resolution and improvement. In summary, continuous improvement methods facilitate the use of data, open discussion, participative decision making, and critical reflection that are the hallmark of excellence in higher education.

NOTES

1. Jim B. Wallace, "The Case for Student as Customer," *Quality Progress* (February 1999): 49.

2. Caroline Fisher and Elizabeth Weymann, "Participative Curriculum Planning." *Journal of Innovative Management* 4, no. 4 (summer 1999).

3. Richard M. Felder and Rebecca Brent, "How to Improve Teaching Quality," *Quality Management Journal* 6, no. 2. (1999): 9–21.

4. Ruth Ash, Amanda Borden, Jack Brymer, David Chapman, Joe Dean, Rosemary Fisk, Marylyn Garvin, Jon Harris, Ron Jenkins, Bill Mathews, Mike

McCormack, Marlene Reed, Don Sandley, Billy Strickland, and Jean Thomason, *Betterment: The Samford Way*. (Birmingham, AL: Samford University, 2002).

5. Joseph O. Dean, Jr., H. Anthony McBridge, Pamela J. Sims, Paula A. Thompson, and Andrew A. Webster, "The Samford Plan: A TQM Process Model for Curriculum Development and Refinement," Samford University Press, 2002.

6. William F. Massey, "Auditing Higher Education to Improve Quality," *Chronicle of Higher Education*, June 20, 2003.

7. "Faculty Explore Excellence in Teaching," *Dialog*, April 2003.

8. Kurt Lewin, *Field Theory in Social Sciences*, Dorwin Cartwright, ed. (New York: Harper & Brothers, 1951).

9. John R. Dew, "Student Attendance Patterns in Large Lecture Classes," National Consortium for Continuous Improvement in Higher Education Conference presentation, fall 2002.

APPENDIX
360 Feedback Process:
Contributors Workbook

FOR ACADEMIC ADMINISTRATORS

Thank you for participating in this feedback process. This process allows administrators to receive feedback from their peers, employees, and stakeholders.

Each person who receives feedback will receive information from a group of people who could be peers in the university, faculty, or staff that the individual supervises, or stakeholders who receive services from this individual. The individual will also receive feedback from his/her manager.

In order to make this feedback process work, it is critical that everyone involved understand the measure of responsibility that he or she is taking on. You will be asked to provide feedback for a designated person on five feedback criteria: Teamwork and Facilitation, Planning and Problem Solving, Compliance/Integrity, Communication and Interpersonal Skills, and Initiative and Leadership Skills. In order to assure consistency in interpreting these feedback criteria, a list of desirable and undesirable qualities has been provided for all the criteria. After reviewing these qualities, you will be asked to select from a numerical scale to describe the individual's behavior in each category. For each category, you will also be provided space to write comments. These comments are a vital part of the process.

It is important to understand that all data will be kept confidential. The administrator receiving the feedback will not see the individual feedback sheets but will receive a form that consolidates all the feedback.

Thank you for taking the time to contribute to the feedback process.

Instructions

This workbook is provided to aid you in providing feedback to an academic administrator. It will further define each of the five feedback criteria that comprise the 360 Feedback Process.

1. This feedback form should be done privately. Care has been taken to keep all information private. When filling out the form, the same confidentiality should be maintained.

2. Do not be in a rush to complete the feedback form. Your feedback is very important to this person. Take the time to read all the information in this workbook.

3. In addition to selecting from the numerical scale, it is vital that you provide written input wherever possible. It is these comments that will be the most important tool in helping the administrator to continue to improve.

4. The last page of this workbook is used as the response sheet. *It is the only* sheet that will be returned to the coordinator.

5. Review the numerical scaling system before you proceed. Each criterion includes examples of desirable and undesirable qualities or behaviors. These examples are **not** meant to be the sole definition of the criteria. They are provided as positive and negative examples of the behavior that describe the criteria.

6. Circle the number for each of the five criteria. Write additional comments in the appropriate area.

7. There is no need to total up or average the numbers. Each of the five criteria is equally weighted.

8. Please complete the feedback form within two days and return it to:

Feedback Definition

Shown below is the numerical scale to use for each of the five feedback criteria. After reviewing the desirable and undesirable qualities for each criterion, plus any other qualities not listed that you feel apply, determine a numerical score. Circle the score on the Feedback Worksheet. To maintain confidentiality, this is the only place the score should be written. The Feedback Worksheet is the only sheet that will be returned. The rest of the workbook is just an aid to help fill out the worksheet.

When reviewing the individual's behaviors in each criterion, the following question should be asked:

How well and to what degree does the administrator demonstrate these qualities?

Level	Description
1	This individual demonstrates an uncompromising level of commitment to all of the qualities that exemplify this criterion. His/her actions serve as a model to the rest of the university.
2	This individual demonstrates many desirable qualities of this feedback criterion. She/he also shows a high degree of commitment to this criterion.
3	This individual frequently demonstrates desirable qualities of this feedback criterion.
4	This person has difficulty exhibiting the qualities that highlight this criterion and often demonstrates undesirable qualities of the criterion.
5	This person rarely demonstrates the desirable qualities of the criteria. He/she more frequently exhibits the undesirable qualities.

Criterion #1: Teamwork and Facilitation

Desirable qualities: This person:

Is able to bring people together to work effectively.

Promotes and demonstrates trust.

Openly shares knowledge, expertise, and goals.

Is able to lead meetings in a way that is focused and effective.

Helps to resolve individual and group conflict.

When appropriate, promotes and demonstrates decisions based on consensus.

Helps to make the people around him/her better.

Is constantly evaluating the process for changes that support the college's goals.

Is willing to collaborate with other groups in and outside the college.

Provides feedback to others in a positive and constructive manner.

Shares information and recognition with others.

Undesirable qualities: This person:

Acts without seeking input or consensus from others.

Has a "get it done no matter who I have to go over" attitude.

Does not recognize or communicate the impact of his/her actions to faculty, staff, students, or other administrators.

Conducts meetings with no clear focus or is not well structured.

Is a source of conflict within the college or department.

Is more concerned with individual success and reward than with meeting college or department goals.

Is not willing to evaluate new methods or process changes.

Is frustrated by having to work in a collegial manner.

Does not provide feedback to others or does it in a way that creates conflict or animosity.

Acts independently of others in the college or department and does not use available resources.

Criterion #2: Planning and Problem Solving

Desirable qualities: This person:

Guides projects and responds to requests in a timely and efficient manner.

Effectively matches people's skills with their assigned tasks.

Clearly defines problems through logical thought processes.

Seeks and uses relevant data to solve problems.

Seeks and uses faculty input to solve problems.

Is focused on the needs of stakeholders.

Uses creative and open-minded approaches to solving problems.

Is able to organize and conduct many tasks in parallel.

Effectively uses the skills of faculty and staff in his/her group.

Assembles all necessary faculty and staff early in a project and assures effective communication of schedules and due dates for everyone.

Effectively communicates lessons learned for future reference.

Undesirable qualities: This person:

Is often unable to determine how or where to start a project.

Does not get the appropriate faculty or staff involved from the start.

Does not communicate the overall goal or task of a project but is content to have people just do assigned duties.

Has trouble identifying the factors causing a problem.

Does not meet commitments and appears to be unfocused toward desired results.

Is not focused on stakeholders' needs.

Overruns his/her budgetary boundaries.

Does not communicate lessons learned.

Criterion #3: Compliance and Integrity

Desirable qualities: This person:

Places high importance on personal integrity.

Ensures that financial records are accurate.

Is conscious and aware of federal and state government requirements, including those concerning research, finances, and personnel.

Places a high emphasis on safety and emphasizes safety to all faculty, staff, and students.

Thoroughly evaluates the environmental impact to individuals and the community for all projects.

Is not afraid to stop a project and consult others when an issue of compliance or integrity is raised.

Treats faculty, staff, students, and alumni with respect, independent of race, gender, religion, nationality, or personal issues.

Shares expertise freely.

Is open to new ideas. Seeks out and utilizes best practices.

Undesirable qualities: This person:

Does not ensure accurate financial records.

Is ignorant of government regulations that apply to his/her position.

Ignores issues related to personnel safety.

Does not bring in appropriate Human Resources, EEO, safety, or environmental staff when a problem is identified.

Expresses prejudice toward others based on race, gender, religion, nationality, or personal issues.

Is closed-minded. Suffers from a "not invented here" attitude.

Makes no effort to expand knowledge base or to stay current.

Criterion #4: Communication and Interpersonal Skills

Desirable qualities: This person:

Tailors his/her communications to the faculty and staff so as to be effective in communicating needs, goals, and status.

Communicates effectively so that people or groups do not duplicate work unnecessarily.

Gives constructive criticism in a method that others are able to understand and build on.

Keeps faculty and staff informed.

Listens to others viewpoints in an objective manner.

Provides positive reinforcement and feedback to individuals and the entire department or college.

Has good written communications.

Has good presentation skills.

Shares appropriate information freely with faculty and staff.

Bases his/her communications on fact and data rather than speculation.

Makes appropriate and effective use of e-mail.

Undesirable qualities: This person:

Has difficulty communicating effectively with others.

Does not communicate his/her needs or intentions to others.

Creates conflict or resentment with others by giving criticism in a non-constructive, sarcastic, or negative manner.

Does not communicate vital information to faculty and staff.

Does not listen to others' ideas or viewpoints.

Rarely, if ever, gives positive reinforcement to others.

Does not easily share information with others and prefers to retain information so as to be considered indispensable.

Is unwilling to share recognition with others.

Bases his/her communication on speculation rather than on facts.

Makes inappropriate and/or ineffective use of e-mail.

Criterion 5: Initiative and Leadership Skills

Desirable qualities: This person:

Willingly takes on new issues and pursues a course of action without hesitation.

Establishes a clear strategic plan for his/her organization.

Consistently ensures contributions from everyone in his/her organization.

Recognizes areas for improvements.

Has open communications that encourages people to discuss and resolve problems.

Clearly and thoroughly evaluates facts and makes appropriate decisions.

Demonstrates the confidence to act on his/her own, yet freely solicits advice and counsel from appropriate resources when required.

Pursues goals and objectives with dedication and enthusiasm.

Accepts responsibility for actions, decisions, and results.

Undesirable qualities: This person:

Does not pursue new assignments on his/her own initiative.

Is indecisive in his/her approach and actions.

Is not supportive of other people in the college or department.

Acts independently of the rest of the college or department.

Does not freely delegate responsibility or seek advice when needed.

Does not recognize or identify problems and needed change.

Lacks dedication and enthusiasm to assigned responsibilities.

Does not seek out information or verify accuracy of data before making a decision.

Is easily discouraged by barriers and is unwilling to try a different approach to reach a solution.

See 360 Feedback Worksheet on the following page.

360 FEEDBACK WORKSHEET Feedback for _____

From: Department Chair   Faculty   Staff Member   Peer   Dean
        or Program Director   (circle one)

Please circle a numerical score and provide written comments for each criteria.

Teamwork and Facilitation   1   2   3   4   5
                                   Outstanding   Unsatisfactory
Comments:

Planning and Problem Solving   1   2   3   4   5
                                   Outstanding   Unsatisfactory
Comments:

Compliance and Integrity   1   2   3   4   5
                                   Outstanding   Unsatisfactory
Comments:

**Communication and
Interpersonal Skills**   1   2   3   4   5
                                   Outstanding   Unsatisfactory
Comments:

Leadership & Initiative   1   2   3   4   5
                                   Outstanding   Unsatisfactory
Comments:

BIBLIOGRAPHY

Adolph, Laurie, and Harriet Howell Custer. "Field Notes from Two Trail-breakers." *A Collection of Papers on Self-Study and Institutional Improvement.* The Higher Learning Commission, Chicago, 2002.

Ash, Ruth, Amanda Borden, Jack Brymer, et. al. *Betterment: The Samford Way.* Birmingham, AL: Samford University, 2002.

Baggett, Mark. "Demythologizing Quality Improvement for Faculty." In *Quality Quest in the Academic Process.* Samford University and GOAL/QPC, 1992.

Bonvillian, Gary, and Terry Dennis. *TQM in Higher Education.* Edited by Serbrenia J. Sims and Ronald R. Sims. Westport, CT: Praeger Publishers, 1995.

Bradford, Leland P., and Ronald Lippitt. "Building a Democratic Work Group." *Personnel* 22, no. 2 (1945).

California State University. "Mapping the Progress of Process Mapping." *Quality Improvement Newsletter.* January 2000.

California State University System. *Quality Improvement Newsletter.* April 2000.

Camp, Robert C. *Benchmarking: The Search for Industry Best Practices that Lead to Superior Performance.* Milwaukee, WI: ASQ Quality Press, 1989.

Center for Quality. Binghamton University. *Partners* 2, no. 1 (2001).

Center for Quality and Planning. *Achieving Goals.* Pennsylvania State University. November 2000.

Coleman, Mary Sue. "Implementing a Strategic Plan Using Indicators and Targets." In *Pursuing Excellence in Higher Education,* edited by Brent D. Ruben. San Francisco: Jossey-Bass, 2004.

Coley, Ron, and Paul K. Diamond. "A Balanced Scorecard for Business and Administrative Services at University of California, Berkeley." In

Pursuing Excellence in Higher Education, edited by Brent D. Ruben. San Francisco: Jossey-Bass, 2004.

Corts, Thomas, and James C. Eck. "Ten Ways to Track Performance." *Trustee Magazine*, January 2002.

Covey, Stephen. *The Seven Habits of Highly Effective People*. New York: Simon & Schuster, 1989.

Crosby, Phillip. *Quality Is Free*. New York: McGraw-Hill, 1979.

Dean, Joseph O., Jr., H. Anthony McBridge, Pamela J. Sims, et. al. "The Samford Plan: A TQM Process Model for Curriculum Development and Refinement." Birgmingham, AL: Samford University, 2002.

Deming, W. Edwards. *Quality, Productivity, and Competitive Position*. Cambridge, MA: MIT Press, 1982.

Dew, John R. *Empowerment and Democracy in the Workplace*. Westport, CT: Quorum Books, 1997.

Dew, John R. "Student Attendance Patterns in Large Lecture Classes." Paper presented at the National Consortium for Continuous Improvement in Higher Education Conference, University of Alabama, fall 2002.

Engelkemeyer, Susan. "Applying Benchmarking in Higher Education." *Quality Management Journal* 5, no. 4 (1998).

Felder, Richard M., and Rebecca Brent. "How to Improve Teaching Quality." *Quality Management Journal* 6, no 2 (1999).

Fisher, Caroline, and Elizabeth Weymann. "Participative Curriculum Planning." *Journal of Innovative Management* 4, no. 4 (summer 1999).

Freire, Paulo. *The Politics of Education*. South Hadley, MA: Bergin & Garvey, 1981.

Gantt, Henry. *Industrial Leadership*. New Haven, CT: Yale University Press, 1916.

Hall, Doug. *Jump Start Your Brain*. New York: Warner Books, 1995.

Higher Learning Commission. *AQIP Quality Criteria*. Chicago, 2001.

Hollis, Harry. "Quality Profile: Belmont University." The Conference Board, July 1997.

Hunsinger, Ronald. "Total Quality Improvement in the Basic Sciences." In *Quality Quest in the Academic Process*. Birmingham, AL: Samford University and GOAL/QPC, 1992.

Ishikawa, Kaoru. *Guide to Quality Control*. Tokyo, Japan: Asian Productivity Center 1976.

Johnson, Bob. "Process Management at UW–Stout." NCCI Conference, 2002.

Juran, Joseph. *Juran on Leadership for Quality*. New York: Macmillan, 1989.

Juran, Joseph. *Managerial Breakthrough*. New York: McGraw-Hill, 1964.

Lehr, Jennifer K., and Brent D. Ruben. "Excellence in Higher Education: A Baldrige-Based Self-Assessment Guide for Higher Education." *Assessment Update* 11, no. 1 (January/February 1999).

Lewin, Kurt. *Field Theory in Social Sciences*. Edited by Dorwin Cartwright. New York: Harper & Brothers, 1951.

Knowles, Malcolm, and Hulda Knowles. *Introduction to Group Dynamics*. New York: Cambridge Press, 1972.

Marsick, Victoria J. "Action Learning and Reflection in the Workplace." In *Fostering Critical Reflection in Adulthood*. Edited by Jack Mezirow. San Francisco: Jossey-Bass, 1990.

Massey, William F. "Auditing Higher Education to Improve Quality." *Chronicle of Higher Education*. June 20, 2003.

Meyer, Christopher. "How the Right Measures Help Teams Excel." *Harvard Business Review*, May–June 1994.

Mezirow, Jack. *Fostering Critical Reflection in Adulthood*. San Francisco: Jossey-Bass, 1990.

Middle States Commission on Higher Education. *Student Learning Assessment: Options and Resources*. Philadelphia, PA, 2003.

Morley, Louise. *Quality and Power in Higher Education*. Berkshire, UK: Open University Press, 2003.

Moseley, Donald C. "Nominal Grouping as an Organizational Development Intervention Technique." *Training and Development Journal*, March 1974.

Nagey, Joanne, et al. "Madison: How TQM Helped Change an Admissions Process." *Change*, May/June 1993.

National Institute of Standards and Technology. *Educational Criteria for Performance Excellence*. Gaithersburg, MD: U.S. Department of Commerce, 2002.

Peters, Thomas J., and Robert H. Waterman. *In Search of Excellence*. New York: Warner Books, 1982.

Porter, Warren P., and Kathleen A. Paris. "Creating a Strategic Plan." Department of Zoology. Madison, WI: The University of Wisconsin–Madison, 1998.

Rasch, Lee. "Quality . . . the Western Way." Achieving and Sustaining Excellence in Higher Education Conference. Menomonie, WI: The University of Wisconsin–Stout, 2002.

Schon, Donald. *The Reflective Practitioner*. New York: Basic Books, 1983.

Sherlock, Barbara. "Teams Improve the Scheduling of Courses, the Handling of SRTE Forms and Audio Visual Support in Classrooms." Center for Quality and Planning, Pennsylvania State University, January/February 2002.

Shor, Ira. *Empowering Education*. Chicago: University of Chicago Press, 1992.

Southern Association of Colleges and Schools. *Principles of Accreditation: Foundations for Quality Enhancement*. Atlanta, GA, 2003.

Sperry, Roger. *Science and Moral Priority*. New York: Columbia University Press, 1983.

Thor, Carl. "A Complete Organizational Measurement System." *International Productivity Journal* (spring 1990).

University of California, Berkeley. *Report of the Chancellor's Exploratory Committee on Continuous Improvement*. Berkeley, CA, 1999.

University of Miami. *Continuous Improvement Update*. Miami, FL, March 2001.

University of Miami Quality Website. "Secret Shopping." April 2002.

University of Michigan. "Survey Results: Perceptions of the Work Environment at Michigan." 1995.

University of Michigan. "Quality in Daily Activities." *M Quality*. Ann Arbor, MI, 1996.

University of Texas. "Quality Center Report." Fall 1998.

University of Wisconsin–Stout. *Application for the Malcolm Baldrige National Quality Award*. Minomonie, WI, 2001.

Villanova University. Quality Activity Report, 2002.

Wallace, Jim B. "The Case for Student as Customer." *Quality Progress*. February 1999.

Warzynski, Chester C. "Leadership Development at Cornell University." In *Pursuing Excellence in Higher Education*, edited by Brent D. Ruben. San Francisco: Jossey-Bass, 2004.

Waters, Lois. *TQM in Higher Education*. Edited by Serbrenia J. Sims and Ronald R. Sims. Westport, CT: Praeger Press, 1995.

Weisbord, Marvin. *Developing Common Ground*. San Francisco: Barrett-Kohler Press, 1992.

Wheatley, Walter. *TQM in Higher Education*. Edited by Serbrenia J. Sims and Ronald R. Sims. Westport, CT: Praeger Press, 1995.

Williams, Susan. "How Quality Improvement Teams Work to Improve Processes in Departments and Academic Units." In *Quality Quest in the Academic Process*. Birmingham, AL: Samford University and GOAL/QPC, 1992.

Willits, Billie S., and Leonard E. Pollack. "Penn State's Excellence in Leadership and Management Program." In *Pursuing Excellence in Higher Education*, edited by Brent D. Ruben. San Francisco: Jossey-Bass, 2004.

Woolridge, Annie. *TQM in Higher Education*. Edited by Serbrenia J. Sims and Ronald R. Sims. Westport, CT: Praeger Publishers, 1995.

Xerox Quality Services. *A World of Quality*. Rochester, NY: XQS Press, 1993.

Yoji, Akao. *Quality Function Deployment*. Cambridge, MA: Productivity Press, 1990.

INDEX

About the Authors

JOHN ROBERT DEW is Director for Continuous Quality Improvement at the University of Alabama, responsible for strategic planning, performance measurement, and process improvement activities across the campus. He is also a member of the graduate school faculty in engineering and business. Dew was formerly Manager for Mission Success at Lockheed Martin Corporation, responsible for management quality improvement initiative and strategic planning activities at the U.S. Department of Energy nuclear facility.

MOLLY McGOWAN NEARING is the Senior Quality Facilitator at the Center for Quality at the State University of New York, Binghamton. She is a charter member of the National Consortium for Continuous Improvement in Higher Education (NCCI) and has served on NCCI's National Conference Planning Committee, the Learning Systems Committee, and currently is the NCCI Program Chair.